To Mickey –
I enjoyed our
dinner – Keep that
smile!

Tales From The Lesson Tee

All the very best

4/27/12

ISBN: 1-4564-9274-8
ISBN-13: 9781456492748

Tales From The Lesson Tee

How to Know Your Game, Know Yourself, and Play Better Without Changing Your Swing

John Kennedy

Westchester Country Club
Director of Golf

2010

Dedication

For my wife Eileen, son John and daughter Sarah, with heartfelt thanks for the many hours—years, even—they have given up so that I could pursue my profession.

CONTENTS

V—IT'S ALL IN THE MIND

VI—FITNESS: A MUST IF YOU WANT TO IMPROVE

VII—TECHNOLOGY

ACKNOWLEDGEMENTS

Learning how to teach golf is an evolving process, a combination of art and science that builds on what has gone before. It has always been clear to me that whatever success I've had as a teacher is based on what I've been able to learn from my fellow professionals, going back to the very first ones when I decided to pursue this instead of the financial career that was my goal as a college student.

There are more professionals then I can count who have contributed to my knowledge base in one way or another, whether through their books or clinics, or by simply observing them at work. Thanks to all of them, but to be more specific, there are a few I have worked closely with who have helped shape my teaching philosophy: Tom Patri, Harvey Lannak, Barry Troiano, Kelley Moser, Gary Weir, Monique Thoresz, Bruce Zabriski, Dave Czaja, Debbie Austin, and two men whose approach to the game is unique and effective—Peter Croker and Howard Wykoff.

Frank (Skip) Latella is the one who convinced me, and many others, of the importance of being physically capable of making a proper swing, and his creation of the Flexor system does a remarkable job of addressing those needs. Thanks to him, as well. Bob Carney, the creative director of Golf Digest, Rick Lipsey of Golf Magazine and Gary Vandeweghe, the former president of the California Golf Association, also deserve my thanks for their suggestions, and Gabe Perle, probably the country's leading intellectual property attorney, was most helpful to the project.

Thanks also to my staff, and to the members of Westchester Country Club, whose support has allowed me the time to follow my path, and also to my students—their desire to improve has gone a long way in helping me not only refine my belief system, but also to validate it.

And finally there is my editor, Leo Levine, who first suggested that my experiences as a teacher could make a difference to a wider circle of golfers if we put this book together. His efforts in organizing my thoughts have been of considerable help.

John Kennedy
Rye, New York
November 2010

EDITOR'S NOTE

John Kennedy is the director of golf at Westchester Country Club in Rye, New York, about 25 miles northeast of midtown Manhattan. It is one of America's larger clubs, both in the size of the membership and in its physical plant, which includes two 18-hole courses, a nine-hole par-three layout and various practice areas for both the long and short games.

The club was created after the close of World War I as the crown jewel of John McEntee Bowman's Biltmore Hotel chain and was something that might have been dreamed up by F. Scott Fitzgerald. At the outset it was the Westchester-Biltmore, "America's Finest Resort," complete with a nine-story hotel, a beach club on Long Island Sound 10 minutes' distant, stables, three polo fields, indoor and outdoor pools, 20 tennis courts and courses designed by U.S. Amateur champion Walter Travis, one of the pre-eminent architects of the era. One had to be a member to own a house on the grounds, which covered more than 600 acres.

Walter Hagen, winner of four British and two U.S Opens and five PGA championships, had a hideout in the hotel, and was a member of the foursome that inaugurated the first course in 1921. He played with home club pro Cuthbert Butchart, two-time PGA champion Long Jim Barnes of nearby Siwanoy Country Club, and the Westchester golf secretary, a tall Scotsman who had lost one eye in The Great War who Bowman brought over to run the golf program in the way such things were done in Britain. He was Tommy Armour, who soon after turned professional, won the U.S. Open and became one of this country's leading instructors. The stock market crash of 1929 marked the end of Bowman's dream, the members took over, and the "Biltmore" half of the name passed into history. The club remains, with the early jazz-era days a distant memory.

Kennedy has been there for 20 years at this writing, and on a scale of one to 10 most of us consider him an 11. Our opinion of him is obviously shared by others, as he is the PGA of America's 2010 Horton Smith Award winner, which means his peers have voted him the nation's leading educator in his profession. That is high praise indeed.

When it comes to his knowledge of the game, his rating is somewhere off the charts. And although John has spent his professional career at private clubs, he grew up, as many of us did, on municipal courses. He knows what it is to wait on line at five in the morning, to play out of dirt-filled bunkers and to putt on greens that have more bumps than flat spots.

In his four decades as a professional he's learned that so-called "classic" methods of golf instruction don't work as well as they should. What he has found, on his way to a number of teaching awards, is that the vast majority of golfers don't make lasting improvements because their concept of the game, and estimate of their abilities, are either incorrect or simply don't exist. What he has done here may surprise a number of teachers, not to mention many golfers, because he is telling us what the realities are. He will give you a number of ways to score better while keeping the swing you already have. One thing it won't do, with a few exceptions, is deal with the technical aspects of the swing. Hundreds of books have been written on this subject but John and his staff know swing instruction is best delivered on a person-to-person basis.

Although all good swings have certain elements in common, "one size" lessons do not, most definitely, fit everyone. But should you want to start the journey to swing improvement, he has included an important section on this most basic element of the game to let you know what you will face in the months and years ahead. If you undertake this, remember, the magic of the game is in the journey. No one is ever completely satisfied. Thirty handicappers would like to be 25's, and Tiger Woods wants to win one more.

In a golfing life that's covered a number of decades and several continents, playing with Jack Nicklaus and Arnold Palmer, Seve Ballesteros and at least 30 other members of the PGA Tour, two basic talents made themselves obvious to me, one of them immediately.

That was ball-striking ability, with Nicklaus, Palmer and company at one end of the spectrum and the great mass of middle and high-handicap amateurs at the other: Some of this came with their DNA, but much was learned through thousands of practice hours.

The other factor, at least as important, showed itself after a few holes: Good golfers seldom make mental mistakes. High-handicap golfers make them all too often. The number of mental errors, in fact, seems to increase in direct proportion to the handicap.

John's senior staff includes head professional Harvey Lannak, director of instruction Gary Weir, Kelley Moser, Barry Troiano and Monique Thoresz, and we asked three of them what an 18's handicap would be if it were possible, in some fashion, to transplant the pro's golfing brain to his—not their swing, just their judgment. Two said 13, one said 14. In other words, you could improve four or five strokes merely by using your head.

Those four or five strokes are here, and somewhere in these pages you can find the key to your own ambitions. That's the fascination of the game. You can always improve, and if not by changing your swing, then by opening your mind, facing reality and realizing you are on the journey of a lifetime, one that will never end, but one that can provide you with much enjoyment on the way.

Leo Levine
Stamford CT
November 2010

INTRODUCTION

John Kennedy and I met in the early 70's at the start of our professional careers, and we've touched many of the same bases and been friends ever since. My first teaching job when I left the University of Houston was at Westchester Country Club, where John has been the director of golf for 20 years now, and one of his early positions was at Sleepy Hollow Country Club overlooking the Hudson River, where some years later I was the head professional before moving south to start my school at Doral.

His career has been a distinguished one, with his "public" high point being named the PGA Horton Smith Award winner for 2010, a national recognition of career-long contributions to PGA of America educational programs. In the New York Metropolitan area John's reputation as an educator and a teacher has been known for years. At this writing, in addition to his more than full-time job running the golf program at one of this country's largest clubs, John is the leader of an ambitious effort that is producing the first-ever "how to" manual for PGA head professionals.

This is a monster project that is best measured in pounds rather than number of pages, and will be a milestone in the ongoing process of establishing performance standards for members of our profession.

But that's down the road. Right here, and right now, John has put together some invaluable information on how to improve your game by opening your mind while living with the swing you have. You might think there is a contradiction here, since my emphasis is on teaching people how to swing better.

Not at all. The two parts are complimentary—a better swing and a better mind have to go together for real long-term improvement. Whether you're a 30 handicapper or scratch, John's got something in here that will help you.

Jim McLean
Miami

UNDERSTANDING THE GAME, UNDERSTANDING YOURSELF

1. WHY WE DON'T IMPROVE

In the 20 years I've been at Westchester our focus has been on improving the golf experience for our members—to raise the standard of play.

I can look back on what we've accomplished with some degree of satisfaction, but at the same time realize we've not been able to lower their handicaps as much as we'd like. This is despite the fact that our teaching staff is one any club would be proud to have, and are busy giving lessons almost literally from sunrise to sunset.

Our group includes six veteran professionals. Five of us are PGA Class A members and one is a Class A member of the British PGA. Our teachers have won sectional and national PGA awards, and we've been on the lesson tee for a combined total of more than 120,000 hours. Our students have ranged from Tour professionals—both PGA and LPGA—to beginners, men and women, juniors and seniors. We've watched thousands of people try to improve, and have not seen the rate of growth you might expect considering the time, effort and expense that's been devoted to this.

And our members, in this regard, are basically no different than golfers everywhere.

Why?

Because the basic approach to instruction is backwards.

In practically every other formalized learning experience the student sets the parameters: He/she decides how much time to invest, chooses the school and pays the tuition.

But the teacher establishes the curriculum, determines the goal and the path to that goal, and conducts periodic reviews along the way.

This rarely happens in golf.

All of us who play, from rank beginners to an Open champion, can be divided into three groups:

- People who play just to enjoy themselves, possibly for the social benefits, and who don't much care what they shoot. They are with their buddies, or play on Wednesday because it is Ladies' Day, and that's fine. They are having fun, and for them that's the goal.
- People who want to improve, but are limited in certain respects—lack of time, money, have physical shortcomings.

- People who want to improve and can commit whatever is required.

If you belong to that first group, then this doesn't apply to you. You're happy with the state of your game, and if you take lessons at all, they are usually few and far between, and probably have the same effect as putting a band-aid on a broken leg.

There's something in this book for you, worth at least a couple of strokes just by getting you to think more clearly.

But if you want to commit to improvement, after you decide on how much time and money you have available, and after you choose a teacher, the teacher is the one who should establish realistic goals and determine your path to improvement. Your teacher is the one who will set up the lesson plan, practice plans, playing plans, physical evaluations, equipment evaluations and the rest.

What you have to do is make the commitment, be realistic in your goals, and understand that the improvement process involves taking many small steps, not one or two gigantic leaps.

What all of us must understand is that we may never be as a good as we would like to be. That is the nature of the game.

The magic, the fascination of golf lies in the journey. Geno Auriemma, the coach of the University of Connecticut's NCAA women's basketball champions, tells his players to seek perfection—which they will never reach, but in seeking it, they will find excellence.

The same can be said for golf.

Whether your handicap is three or 30, if you want to improve, remember—improvement is an ongoing process and you have to make the process fun. When the process is enjoyable, you are likely to stay on the path you have set—and are more than likely to achieve your goal.

We can always get better.

2. THE PAST AND THE FUTURE

Usually, with the best of intentions, you started with a goal of improving. It was just "a goal," not a clearly defined one.

You took lessons, or read a book and/or watched the Golf Channel, you may have invested in new equipment, or you may have started an exercise program.

You may have done all or part of this a number of times.

Initially you improved, like when you re-grip your irons or change putters. But too often, at the end of the season, all of your investment in time and money did not translate itself into the result you expected.

Be honest with yourself: Did you have a plan, or just a desire?

Don't feel guilty, or misinformed. Today's teaching professionals are better trained and have more tools available (e.g., video, launch monitors) than ever before. And you spent a lot of time and money.

But did you understand what would be involved?

Were you and your teacher on the same wavelength? Did you have an in-depth discussion with your teacher before you started? Did you have periodic evaluations of your progress?

The National Golf Foundation, which tracks the state of the game, tells us there are approximately 27 million golfers in America, with two million of that number—a decided minority—belonging to private clubs and the rest playing at resort, daily fee or municipal courses. Approximately 15 million of the total are considered "core" golfers. An estimate from the nation's largest handicap service tells us that for those players who are active enough to post scores, the current average men's handicap is 17 or 18, depending on the difficulty of the course, and the women's average is about 32.

Two decades earlier these numbers were two strokes higher. So despite the great advances in equipment, instruction and course conditioning over the past 20 years, most of us haven't improved that much. This holds true for both private club and public-course players.

There are three reasons for this:

- Instruction that is ineffective because the player does not practice the "correct" information on a consistent basis. He will stick with the new information for as long as he likes the results, but will start searching for a different tip once undesirable ball striking resumes.

- Lack of proper information, which could be bad instruction, or more often no instruction at all. So if you are ready to find a teacher, make sure he or she is someone who knows their subject, and who is on your wavelength when it comes to communicating.
- Instruction, for the most part, is confined to the swing, rather than showing you how to manage your way around the course.

Most players, National Golf Foundation research tells us, have modest ambitions when it comes to improvement—something on the order of three or four shots.

Avoid the many detours most golfers take—information overload, irregular practice routines, and so on. Stay on a straight path—keep yourself, not just your ball, in play.

I'm sure there is something in these pages that will save you those three or four strokes, hopefully even more. That's the magic of golf: We can always get better.

And we can learn to enjoy the journey.

3. THE EDUCATION OF A TEACHER

Our family had moved to a house just below Brooklawn Country Club in Fairfield, Connecticut, and when I was 12, I went up the hill and started caddying to make some money, because you needed to fend for yourself in a family of eight children. This was in 1962, and it was quite a sight, since it was before there were many golf carts and everyone took a caddie. There were probably a hundred caddies in the yard and I remember not getting out for almost a month, and eventually my mother, unbeknownst to me, called a neighbor who was a member and arranged for him to ask for me.

So it was a Saturday morning, and I was sitting in the back of the yard when the caddie master called out "Kennedy," and one of the older kids said "What the heck's he doing?" I got my bag, at that time it was three dollars for a round and the tip was 50 cents, so it was $3.50 for a round, but he gave me $3.25. I was happy with my first loop, and I went home and my mother said "How did you do?" I said I got out—even though she knew I was going to—and I said I got $3.25 and she went to the phone and gave the neighbor a piece of her mind.

Growing up caddying was what inspired me to play, and for my eighth grade graduation my father gave me a set of 3-5-7-9 Mike Souchak MacGregor clubs in a red plaid bag and off I went into what has become a lifetime of playing and learning, and learning how to teach.

We played on Mondays, the traditional caddies' day at Brooklawn, and we'd go out early and you could play two rounds if you wanted, but the real education came when my friends and I played at Fairchild Wheeler, known to all as "The Wheel," the public course in our area.

The Wheel was the crucible. It was populated by low-handicappers and if you wanted to be part of the action, you had to be a player. By age 15 our handicaps were all below five, even without any lessons. The great Julius Boros, the two-time U.S. Open winner who grew up at The Wheel, never won the club championship. That's how tough the competition was.

I met him when I was 13, on a sleepy summer Tuesday afternoon when I was the only caddy left in the yard at Brooklawn. The caddy master called me up and there was this Wilson staff bag that was as big as I was and he said "You'll caddy for him."

"Him" was Boros.

I took him down to the range, which was a skating rink in the winter, and there was an ice house in the middle of it, and he said "How far is that building?

"About 140 yards."

Then he asked "How far is the chimney?" and I said "145 yards."

"Give me an eight iron," he said, and he hit the chimney on his first shot.

When we got to the first hole, a dogleg left, he had a second shot of about 155 yards and he asked "What club should I use?" When I caddied for members, 155 yards was a pretty long shot, so I said "Five iron?"

He said "No, seven iron."

So I caddied for the 18 holes, and I had never seen anything like it. That was 1963, the year he won the second of his two Opens, so I caddied for the Open champion and didn't know it.

Boros was an accountant in neighboring Bridgeport until he was 29, then he turned pro in 1949 and three years later won the Open for the first time. Before he was done Boros won 18 Tour events, was on four Ryder Cup teams, and in 1968 became the oldest, at 48, to win the PGA championship.

For someone who has spent most of his career as a teacher and who almost from day one studied the classic methods of making a proper swing, the teen-age years at The Wheel were an invaluable lesson, because they were a graphic demonstration of the fact that getting the ball in the hole is more important than how you do it. The name of the game is "How Many," not "How."

One of the better players was a butcher from Bridgeport who was in his mid-50's and who was a bona fide one handicap, and he'd play skins games with guys who'd average three or four birdies for nine holes. They'd play $20 skins, which back in the mid-60's was a lot of money for public-course players. Their style was different; they'd grab the club with a strong grip since the ground was hard, so in this way they could hit a hook, and they usually had abbreviated backswings but obviously good fundamentals to the extent that they could move the ball. They had choppy putting strokes because the greens were very bumpy, but they had the ability to focus when they needed to, and the ability to pull the trigger.

I was studying the golf swing and what I thought was the right way to do it, and then I watched these guys, who forced you to make a score. You had to make a score or go home, so you learned, at 16 or 17, to shoot 75 or lower if you wanted to play with them.

On the day I graduated from high school my father gave me $100 as a present, and since the ceremony wasn't until that evening I went up to The Wheel looking for game. I was the captain of my Fairfield Prep team, a two handicap, and had just been awarded a golf scholarship to the University of Minnesota, and I ran into Andy Taylor, one of The Wheel's regulars, a factory worker from Bridgeport who played cross-handed.

I shot 34 for the nine and my $100 was gone. Taylor shot 30.

There is more than one way to get the ball in the hole.

4. THE SEARCH FOR THE PERFECT SWING

In 1968, after the game had been played for several centuries, The Golf Society of Great Britain published the first scientific examination of what actually happens during a swing[1]. That marked the start of technology's influence on golf, a game that despite all the advances in equipment over the past 50 years, is still played by feel.

And there is a perfect swing for everyone, although yours may not look like Tiger Woods' or Ben Hogan's. There is one for you, depending on your physical capabilities and your talent level.

Our preoccupation with the swing has tended to obscure the fact that perfect, when it comes to golf, really means getting the ball into the hole in the least possible number of strokes. Take the PGA Tour, for example. Here are roughly 200 of the world's best players, who do this for (hopefully) a living and spend their days practicing.

Yet in competition, as a group they hit fewer than two thirds of the fairways and their greens-in-regulation average is also less than 65 per cent. It would appear "perfect" is a word that should not be connected with golf—until you see the Tour scoring average for the year. It is almost a full stroke under par.

The secret lies in combining whatever swing you have with your ability to play the game, to think your way around the golf course, to react positively to bad breaks, to make good things happen.

The search for perfection is an ongoing one. It never ends, but there is fun and satisfaction in the journey. I've given lessons to men in their 90's who were still searching for that special swing key. It is a game for a lifetime.

And even if you might never get there, know you are in good company. Hogan once said that if he hit two or three shots per round properly, he would consider it a decent effort.

5. ARE YOU WHAT YOU SHOOT?

In the end, it doesn't make any difference if you reached that par five in two, or drove it past your buddies six times. The number that counts is the one you have after 18 holes.

Before we go any farther, a nod in the direction of Dr. Bob Rotella, the nationally-known sports psychologist, who reminds us that shooting a low round does not make you a better person, nor does playing in the mid-90's (or higher) make you a bad one. Golf is a game, and your life's value should have more importance.

That being said, getting to the lowest number possible, after you take your talent level into account, is going to require a number of things, including:

- Checking your ego at the first tee.
- Accepting the fact that you are going to make mistakes. Golf is like life. We all make mistakes, the secret lies in how we correct them.
- Accepting bad breaks. Golf is not a fair game.

- Remembering that golf is played between the ears. Think your way around the course.

- Enjoy the journey. A lot of other people are tied to their jobs today, while you are out with your friends, the sun and the green grass, and the hope that today will be your day.

And when it's over for the day you'll have some memories, a few stories, and a number. Whether that number is 70, or 80, or 106, you'll have all sorts of explanations as to why it wasn't lower—missed a few five-footers or took two in a bunker—but it doesn't make any difference. That's what you shot.

Have you ever heard anyone explain why their number wasn't higher?

6. THE QUICK FIX

Our title includes the phrase "How to get better," a device used by many books in order to attract the reader. Since we would all like to get better at something, the idea that a book might help you fulfill your dreams is always appealing. We even included "without changing your swing" which you might think is an additional sales pitch.

Not so.

The thrust of what you find here is to demonstrate that there are many things you can do to improve **without** changing your swing.

But first you have to realize that I—or any other PGA Professional—can't make you a better golfer. Only you can make yourself a better golfer.

I can tell you what to do and show you what to do, but in the end you have to do it.

There is no Quick Fix.

If you are someone whose scores are in the 100-110 range, a competent professional can get you below 100 with a short conversation about your decision-making process, your ball position and your too-frequent use of a driver.

But are you going to do it?

If you are a mid-to-high 70's player, your chances of getting to the low 70's—depending on your available time—are probably better, because you already know what it takes to improve.

And if you are one of those who says he doesn't care what he shoots, is there any point in reading the rest of this?

Yes, because fewer strokes equal more fun. We know this from experience—everyone's experience. But if you don't have the time or inclination to practice please do NOT take just one lesson, or try to change your swing after reading a magazine or watching a television show. This almost always leads to frustration and no long-term improvement.

Instead, keep on reading. You'll find out how to stretch before playing, how to make realistic decisions, how to breathe to reduce tension and free up your swing—and all sorts of things that will help you enjoy your time on the course without any additional practice.

7. DO YOU NEED A GOAL?

Everyone who picks up a club should have a goal. It can be anything from winning the U.S. Open to beating your friends next Saturday, but having a goal will make the game more interesting, and if you achieve it, that can give you a great deal of satisfaction.

Your goal might be to break 100, or 80, or to hit more fairways, or to cut three strokes from your handicap. But once you have a goal, think about the best way to achieve it.

Whenever I get a new pupil who is interested in serious improvement, the first thing I do is evaluate his present game, and then ask him about his goals. A few years ago I had a successful businessman who was a 20 handicap and said his goal was to be a 10. I told him that this would take at least three hours of practice per week, plus playing twice a week.

He didn't have the time for all that, he said. The lessons would have to do it. There was no way he could do this, considering the time he had available, and we parted, hopefully as friends. In other words, when you choose a goal, make it one that's attainable. And when you reach that plateau, pick another one. You'll be surprised at the progress you can make.

Having the goal of winning the Open wasn't meant as a joke. Right now there are kids in all parts of this country, on dusty munis, who are on the putting green and fantasizing about the next one being "for the Open."

In the years to come one or two of them will make it, and when they do they'll remember their childhood dreams.

Goals are good.

8. SETTING A GOAL

If you are an 18-handicapper, your first goal should be something on the order of becoming a 15, or even a 14. You can have the ultimate goal of being a scratch player, or close to that, but start out with a more realistic target.

The U.S. Golf Association considers an 18 to be the average for male golfers who maintain their handicap on a regular basis, and if you are the USGA's "average man," then you can achieve that first goal in reasonably short order. At this level, a two or three-shot improvement can come just by making fewer mental mistakes.

To get to single digits you'll have to improve your ball striking, but that will come later. Stay in the present, and work on those two or three shots.

Don't forget, the magic is in the journey.

9. HOW TO DEVELOP A PLAN

Establish the goal.

It can be one of two things—either better scores, or better ball striking. They are not necessarily one and the same.

If the goal is lower scores, you have to evaluate all phases of your game:

- Fairways hit—more specifically, number of greens you had legitimate chances to hit from your position in the fairway.
- Greens in regulation—and distances of first putt (How good is your iron game?)
- 50 yards and in—the short game
- Sand play
- Putting
- And perhaps most important, your on-course decision making.

After you've done that, and one way to do it is to rate each of the above on 1-to-10 scale, with 10 being the best, identify your primary weakness, set up a lesson and practice schedule for the next 30 days, and re-evaluate after that time period.

If the goal is better ball striking, your evaluation list should include:

- Your equipment
- Your physical condition
- Your swing mechanics, in both fixed (address, alignment, posture) and in-motion segments

Calculate the amount of time and money you can invest, and establish a realistic course of action. Then re-evaluate after two to four weeks, depending on your progress. If you're not making the desired improvement, discuss it with your professional.

10. IDENTIFY YOUR WEAKNESS

Psychiatry tells us the first step to solving problems is realizing that we have them, and in one sense golf is similar: If you want to improve, the first step is to find out just what needs improvement.

Here are the most common problems seen in over three decades as a teacher, which should be helpful in identifying what part of your game needs help the most. Once you've identified your primary weakness you'll know what to work on first.

- Poor pre-round preparation, practice habits, on-course decisions.
- Over-estimate ability.
- Underestimate problem areas of the course
- Over-estimate average distance you hit each club
- Poor lag putting
- Negative self-image talk while playing
- Using pitching clubs that have less loft than the shot requires
- Allowing the course and/or fellow players to frustrate you
- Poor club selection on tee shots
- Don't recognize when you don't "have it" on a particular day
- Don't make the best of a bad ball-striking day.

Once you start comparing your game to this list you may find more than one problem that needs fixing. If so, then make your own list, giving each a priority. And if you happen to find a lot of them apply to your game, just remember the old saying about how to eat an elephant: One bite at a time.

11. FIND A TEACHER

If you belong to a private club your first choice will most probably be your home professional, but if for some reason you aren't comfortable with him then look elsewhere. Many clubs allow their teaching staffs to take a limited number of non-member pupils. You can contact the PGA of America (PGA.com) for a list of professionals in your area, and there is always the phone book.

You can go to a municipal or daily-fee course, you can talk to your friends who are taking lessons—there are many ways to find one.

A word of caution: Just because someone is a big-name professional at a prestigious club doesn't necessarily mean he is a good teacher, and just because someone is the pro at a nine-hole public course that has pull carts doesn't mean he is a bad teacher.

It's sort of like looking for a doctor; if you have a friend who has a teacher who is good and available and you want to go and start taking lessons from him, that's great. If you don't, you might go to two professionals, so you have a frame of reference before making a decision. If you've never had formal instruction before, or its been a long time since you have, you might not know if that first lesson was good or bad. But if you go to two, or even more, you will have a better chance of finding someone who is pushing the right buttons.

It could be a personality thing, it could be a tone of voice, the speed at which they give you information, it could be the information they give you, or something else. But if you don't have someone who can point you to a professional, take your time in making a decision, because you are going to be spending a lot of time and money with whomever you select.

12. TALK FIRST, SWING LATER

Your first meeting should be a sit-down session without a club, because the pro needs to get to know you, and you need to know him. Spending a half-hour lesson fee for this encounter is much more valuable than going to a range and starting to hit balls, because the professional needs to know what your goals are and how much time you have. You need to be clear about that before you go.

He has to understand you're not looking for a band-aid for a broken leg, you are looking for a long-term commitment, and that will govern the manner in which he approaches your improvement program.

You don't want to go to someone who starts changing your grip and your setup when you're only going to take two lessons that whole summer. If that's all you can afford, or if you're too busy, or you have family demands on your time, you need to be clear: How much time can you spend practicing—which can involve hitting balls, or practicing in front of a mirror at home, but determining these factors before you go to the teacher will help develop a plan.

If you're going to take a lesson every two months I don't think you have the right to call the pro twice a week to ask questions, but if you're going to take regular lessons—regular lessons to me would be every two weeks—you should be able to call him and ask a question. Both of you should be comfortable with that, so establish that in your first meeting. I think it is important for the relationship to know that he's there to help you and not to have to wait two weeks while you're operating under a possible misconception or struggling with a concept the pro can clear up in a sentence or two.

So now you've got your pro, you've got your plan and you're ready to go.

The purpose of all this is to develop what we can call a "belief system," a concept that you can buy into totally. You can't pick and choose between your pro, tips from magazines and the Golf Channel.

13. PAYING ATTENTION

When I was in my early 20's and still developing my teaching skills, I had a winter job in Florida at the club where Bob Toski, perhaps the pre-eminent celebrity instructor of that era, was in residence and occupying one end of the lesson tee.

Toski had what was practically a national list of pupils, many of them big names in either industry or entertainment, while I was struggling at the other end of the range, getting five dollars per lesson and learning how to maintain a student's interest for the entire hour. At the same time, I kept watching Toski's pupils hanging on his every word.

One day I asked him how he did it.

"When it's costing $100 an hour," he laughed, "they pay attention."

14. HOW LONG WILL IT TAKE?

It takes a while. Now how do you define "a while?"

Is that an hour? A week? A month? A year?

It depends on how you learn to learn. That is the key if you are to make progress.

It depends on how clear your mind is, how patient you are with yourself, and the interval between practice sessions.

It might take four one-hour sessions to develop feel for a particular part of a full swing, and if you schedule those sessions every other day, you'll probably get it done in 10 days.

But if you schedule one per week, it might not happen in a month, and it might take more than four sessions because there's too much time in between.

Something has to change with your practice routine if something is going to change with your golf swing.

Despite the popular phrase, there is no such thing as muscle memory. Your brain controls your movements, and your brain has been programmed through thousands of swing repetitions—on the range, on the course. So we have to re-program it for the correct movement patterns. The best possible way to do this is in a low-stress, high-result atmosphere, in which small successes repeated and repeated lead to greater success.

First, you need to identify the areas of your swing that need to be addressed. Then you address each area individually with a practice swing or drill that teaches your brain the correct movement.

Then repeat it—again, and again.

If you take at least two and preferably four correct practice swings between shots you will be on your way to total swing improvement.

At the outset, practice with half-swings at half speed. Your body is easier to control at slower speeds, and you're more likely to make the proper movements.

That's part of it. The other part, which is somewhat revolutionary when it comes to golf instruction, is to do the heavy lifting, the thinking, during your practice swings. Then, when it comes to hitting the ball, just leave it alone—have no mechanical thoughts when you're over the ball.

The example we use is to compare this to teaching a 16-year-old to drive a car. Would you just toss him the keys, climb into the passenger seat and tell him to drive at 60? No way!! He has no feel for the throttle, the brakes or the steering. He has to develop all these at much lower speeds.

But people listen to the description of a golf swing and then go out with a six iron and try to make a swing change at 50, 60 or 70 miles an hour. It's just not going to happen, and so what ends up happening is that you hit bad shots, you get frustrated and you think you're either uncoordinated or dumb, when neither is the case.

The body cannot absorb information at that speed and in this kind of a stress-filled situation, yet people expect to take this new information and go play with it, which even doubles the stress they experienced on the range. Then they wonder why it didn't work, so they think either the lesson was flawed or they are uncoordinated.

The basic problem is the manner in which the program was designed—if it was designed at all. It was doomed to fail because the student's expectations were unrealistic.

So there we have the opening: To improve you need three things—knowledge, feedback and an approach that will allow repetition.

15. NICK'S SWING PLANE

I was speaking with Nick Price's teacher a while back and he described to me the amount of time the two spent on Nick's swing plane one day before the start of a Senior Tour season.

They went to the range at nine in the morning and videotaped him hitting two balls. Then they went inside, in front of a mirror, and made practice swings until lunch—two hours and 45 minutes without hitting a ball, just going through practice swing positions.

"We had to swing maybe 300, 400 times over three hours before he finally felt it," his teacher said, "and then we went out after lunch, and videotaped him again. He was close, so we went back in for an hour, and then went back out." In the course of eight hours Price hit maybe 40 balls.

And Price, in his 50's, is still one of the world's great players.

Most people just want to whack balls, and what they are doing is reinforcing bad habits. So as a corollary to having a learning style, you have to understand that your body cannot learn at top speed. It is just not going to work. Most people don't want to do this, they want to go out and play—which is fine as long as you understand that your swing won't change at "game speed" on the course.

16. ANOTHER VIEWPOINT

Gary Weir is our director of instruction, and he knows there is no quick and easy path to success.

"When people ask me how long it takes," he says, "I tell them it takes as long as it takes. Patience is not a virtue, it is a necessity."

"Golfers who do well," he adds, "are the ones who are patient enough to go and work on the things I want them to work on, and they have to be persistent. If it doesn't work on the second shot, they'll have to keep trying.

"One of the problems I have when I'm coaching someone is to make them patient and persistent. I've had many students who come to me and say 'I really want to get better. I don't like the way I'm playing. I'm a high handicap and I want to improve dramatically. I'll do whatever it takes. You tell me what I've got to do and I'll do it.'

"Then I'll look at his swing and say 'You've got to do this, you've got to do that, you may have to change this...'

"And literally, on the second shot he hits with his new swing, he'll say 'That doesn't work. Why is it hooking now instead of slicing?'

"I had one young man who was hitting maybe 30 per cent of his shots the way he should, with the action he should have.... But he was getting very frustrated with 30 per cent. I keep on telling people an improvement on 30 per cent is 31 per cent, then 32 per cent—it won't go from 30 to 70, not without some work, and not without patience.

"If you give me a 30-handicapper with good athletic ability," Gary says, "He's the easiest person to get better, I can get him significantly better very quickly, but as the handicap goes down it will take more work—and patience."

II—MAKING PROGRESS

17. MORE EDUCATION

When I was going through the final stages of becoming a PGA Class A professional in the mid-1970's, one of the steps included attending a lecture on the methodology of teaching. Jim Flick, one of the country's better-known instructors then and now, was the speaker.

"If I could give back the money to all of the students I taught in my first 10 years," he said, "it would probably be the right thing to do." What he was referring to was that as a young teacher you have all this information, but you have to develop the ability to give the information in the correct sequence.

Instruction is really two things, and the first is developing a chemistry with the student. That's the key, because if somebody's not comfortable you're not going to be able to communicate. The second is being able to identify what they want, and if you can pick that up early on, you're going to be successful. As a young teacher, you assume everybody wants to learn everything you know, and so you give them too much information. As you become more experienced you realize that people's goals are much less lofty than yours. They don't all want to become 10 handicaps if they're a 30. Maybe they just want to be a 28, or maybe they just want to hit a wedge without shanking.

I would say "Less is Better," and the information you give the student has got to be targeted to his or her current condition, be it their physical or their talent level. And you have to remember that people are not going to get better unless they really want to get better. You see that in juniors, you see that in average players—people say they want to get better, but the fact of the matter is they don't practice enough, or they don't pay attention to their improvement plan.

That's hard for some people to admit.

18. GREAT EXPECTATIONS

Flick's advice was never more appropriate than the time I got so far "out in front" of my students that it was embarrassing to all of us. I was teaching at Sleepy Hollow Country Club in the Hudson Valley and one day I had three new ladies scheduled for a group lesson on our par three course, so when the appointed time came I had their bags loaded onto carts and I took off in my cart, headed for the first tee.

When I got there I took a few practice swings, and waited. When they didn't show up after five minutes, I headed back to the staging area. They were there, sitting in the carts.

"Ladies," I said, "we need to get started," and one of them said "John, you forgot to tell us how to start the carts."

19. HOW TO LEARN

Let's assume you have a plan and you have someone helping you. So you're past those two hurdles. The question is how do you take that information and make it worthwhile.

The first thing: You have to have confidence in your teacher.

If you're just out there in a trial-and-error mode it's not going to work. You have to believe that what your teacher is saying is correct for you, and you have to commit to it.

It's like going to a doctor: If you don't have confidence in him you're probably not going to follow through on the therapy. Let's say you have a shoulder injury and the doctor says you have to do the exercises for six weeks, and you do them for a week and it hurts, so you decide I'm not going to do that any more—it hurts. You have to believe in the person with whom you're working.

So let's assume you have a teacher and you have faith in what he says, and you have a plan. The next step, and this is important, is that both you and the teacher know how you learn.

People learn in a variety of ways: Some learn verbally, some learn visually, and some people learn kinesthetically. You have to identify your best method—are you better off feeling something, are you better off hearing something, or are you better off seeing something?

Some people can learn across all three modes but one is usually dominant. Some people learn almost all visually and words go in one ear and out the other. So you have to try all three. You may know going in, but try all three anyway. Look at a videotape and see whether that's helpful. Some people are intellectual and tend to work best off of what they hear, and some have to be pushed around—you have to touch their shoulders, touch their knee, move their hips, move their arms or their hands.

So identify your learning style, and use that throughout the learning process.

20. FIX ONE THING AT A TIME

Every golfer has issues—with setup, with backswing, with down-swing. But if you try to change too many things during a single practice swing you are unlikely to achieve any real improvement.

We can divide the swing into two categories, the preparation stage and the action stage. The preparation stage includes how you grip the club and how you stand, and the action stage is how you swing. The action stage can be broken down into backswing and downswing.

You can effectively make two preparation changes and add one swing key to a single shot. And you must insure that your changes compliment each other—a weaker grip and a more upright back-swing, for example, are two thoughts that fight each other when you attempt to execute them in the same swing.

When you approach a problem, and almost everyone has any-where from two to six or seven really obvious problems in their whole package—you can work on a couple of pre-swing items because you are not in motion while treating these. When it comes to the swing itself, you have to consider yourself either a backswing person or a downswing person for a particular series of balls, because that's the most efficient way to bring about improvement.

When you achieve repetition working on one thing at a time, you have a chance to solidify your habit pattern. If you're working on two swing keys at the same time, you are dividing your attention and your improvement progress will be that much slower.

You can work on several parts of setup and swing in one practice session, but when you're over the ball, don't overload.

21. TIGER SPEAKS

We have a peculiar need to make successful athletes into larger-than-life heroes, probably because most of us live our lives vicariously, and by deifying a winner of one contest or another we somehow gain a connection. Red Smith, the great sports columnist of the 20th century, called the process "Godding them up," and years later this is still the best definition of the process.

In one of the years when Tiger Woods was playing in the Tour tournament at Westchester the players, and particularly Tiger, always tried to avoid crowds, because if they get stuck in a crowd it could be for an hour or two—the crowd would never end, and they would have to be signing autographs instead of heading for the practice tee. So some of the players, when they came off the 18th hole, would dart through the pro shop to avoid the crowds around the putting green.

One day I was standing on the steps in front of the shop and Tiger was coming in. There was a spectator standing near me and as Tiger ran up the steps he bumped into the man and then went through to the locker room.

The man's wife came back a minute or two later, and the first thing he said was "He spoke to me."

"Who spoke to you?" she asked.

And in a tone that indicated he'd seen some sort of ghost, he said "He spoke to me, Tiger Woods spoke to me."

She looked at him, and they were both smiling, and then she asked "What did he say?"

"'Get out of the way. "

22. MAKING A BASIC CHANGE

If you are serious about wanting to make basic changes in your swing, then welcome to the Great Journey on which every golfer, from Old Tom Morris and Harry Vardon, from Hogan and Nicklaus to Tiger and you, has traveled. You will never reach the end of the road, but neither has anyone else.

The "end" is almost immaterial. The journey is what counts.

Woods is reported to be a plus-8 handicapper at his home course, and there's no doubt he wants to be a plus 10. And if your goal is to get from 18 to 14, that's fine. The magic is in the journey. The secret is staying with it and not losing sight of your goal.

Much of what you read here will look familiar, as the steps involved in changing your basic swing are much the same as those you took to fix minor ailments. The principal difference is that now you're taking a more holistic view.

Once you've made the decision you have to do several things:

- Find a teacher and develop a concept
- Have a "Belief System" and stick with it
- Have a feedback system
- Learn how you learn
- Develop an approach that allows repetition.
- Understand the time involved

The concept is the foundation stone. Probably 75 per cent of all golfers lack a concept of what it takes to make a proper swing; they're working without a clear idea of what they should be doing, so the first thing you have to do is assemble your knowledge package, which can come from a variety of sources. Having a competent teaching professional is the most obvious method, but you might not have access to a teacher or perhaps you can't afford one.

There are documented cases of people who have been successful just through reading instructional books and working on their own. U.S. Open and PGA titleholder Larry Nelson did it by reading Ben Hogan's "Five Lessons: The Modern Fundamentals of Golf[2]" when he was in his early 20's, and from start to breaking 70 took only nine months. Granted, he didn't do much else except practice from morning 'till night, but he proved it can be done.

23. KEEP A DIARY

If you are serious about improving, one of the more important tools you can have is a diary—a written record of what you did and how you did each time you played. There are a number of record-keeping systems available on the internet—Google can find them for you—with one of the more sophisticated being ShotbyShot.com. There are also printed forms if you want to maintain your records on paper.

Do your record-keeping within a few hours of having played, when your memory of the round is still fresh. It will only take a few minutes to write down fairways hit, greens in regulation, number of putts and the rest. Then, after five or 10 rounds, you'll have a good idea as to what part of your game needs improvement.

I would also record your practice sessions—approximate number of balls per category—short irons, mid-irons, fairway/rescue clubs, tee shots, chips/pitches, sand play, and so on.

Review your diary weekly and see if your practice matches your game's needs.

The numbers don't lie.

24. THE SWEATER

One day a new pupil showed up, complete with a 30 handicap and a gift certificate from his wife for some lessons. As I usually do with a new player, I asked him what his thoughts were when it came to making a swing. He gave me five concepts, all of which were diametrically opposed to everything I taught.

"Look," I said, "If we are going to make any real progress, you're going to have to forget those things and we'll start from scratch, and it's going to be a slow process."

His face fell, and then I had a thought. "On the other hand," I said, "if you're not happy with that, I'll trade you for one of the best sweaters in the pro shop."

He thought about it for a moment, and said "I'll take the sweater."

25. BARRIERS TO IMPROVEMENT

There are two principal reasons some people don't make progress:

1. Lack of a plan.

You need a clear idea of what it takes to improve. You must understand how many parts there are in a good improvement plan. Obviously there is the swing itself, but then there is the practice plan, the commitment of practice time, there is physical conditioning, equipment, course management, and the ability to evaluate the strengths and weakness of your game.

Most people don't sit down and in a rational fashion review the current state of their game and think "How am I going to improve?"

That's your starting point. You have to have a plan, even if you're a beginner and your goal is to break 100, you have to have a plan. If you want to get better you can't just go out there, swat balls at a driving range, or sign up for a round with your buddies and expect to improve, because it's not going to happen.

There are too many variables in the swing, too many variables in what goes into hitting a driver or striking a chip properly, and if you don't have some kind of guidance or some plan you're going to be spinning in circles, which is probably what at least 50 per cent of the people who pick up a club do, and play that way for 20 or 30 years. They may call it fun, but their level of enjoyment would increase if their game improved.

2. Lack of information or misapplication of the information they have.

People who have a plan but don't have a mentor, or people who are either getting wrong information or are not consistent in the application of the information they have.

When I watch most golfers, I can tell why they're struggling by their answers to two or three key questions:

- What's your concept of the swing?
- What's your thought process?
- Tell me what you do in a typical week.

At that point it's easy to understand why they are where they are.

Back to the basics: You need a plan, and if you do have a plan, does your plan have the right information, and if your professional has given you the right information, are you practicing on a regular basis? There are times when I'll speak with one of our teachers about a particular student and ask him what the player should be working on.

Then I'll ask the player. The two answers are like one of them speaking English, the other Greek. So either the information is not being transmitted properly, or the student isn't hearing it, or he's hearing it, and after a few bad shots he's open to suggestions from his 25-handicap buddy.

Or he'll watch the Golf Channel, and what the TV pro says seems to make sense, and he thinks "OK, I'll try that," even though it doesn't necessarily apply to him, either because of his limited physical ability or his current talent level.

26. AM I IMPROVING?

So let's assume you have the knowledge, now you need some feedback. Again, the preferred solution is to have a teacher. If you don't, a golfing buddy or your wife can help—if you're working on a specific movement and can describe to them **exactly** what the movement should be, they can be your practice mentor. They can say yes, or no, whatever the case might be, and you'll get some feedback.

Another great feedback mechanism, obviously, is videotape. If you can tape your swing, by all means do it. If you can't, then use a mirror, which can be very helpful.

The next step is understanding how long it will take to develop new neural paths in the brain through making consistently correct movements. If you're going to change, make the commitment to the time it takes to make consistently correct swings (with and without a ball) to develop the correct brain paths.

27. SHE IMPROVED, HE DIDN'T

When I first came to Westchester, a lady who was in her early 70's stopped in to see me. She was a nine-hole player whose average score was in the mid 50's, which was not bad for a woman of her age. She had an athletic background, but she'd had some injuries and severe osteoporosis and she no longer had full mobility. You might think she would hardly be a candidate for improvement.

But she said she wanted to commit herself to golf, since she couldn't play tennis any more. She said she'd like to take a lesson a week, and over the period of about a season and a half, we did, probably, ten lessons one season and five lessons the next.

By the middle of the second season her average score was in the mid-40's. That is a 20 or 25 per cent improvement.

She not only took lessons, but she practiced three times a week on her own. I was her only teacher, and I think that is so important, because in that way she only had one source of information, she focused on what I asked her to do, she developed a repetitive swing, and she had the commitment to do this three times a week. In addition to practice, she played twice a week.

Over the next 10 years she won the ladies' nine-hole club championship eight times,. She was a great example of someone who was not in their physical prime, but who had ambition, had a program, and had one source of information.

The other side of the coin is a member who came to me, and eventually went to every teacher on the staff at some point. He was in his mid 60's, very athletic, very strong, who took lessons from everyone.

He took lessons from our professionals, he took lessons from the range staff, he took lessons from the 25-handicapper who happened to walk past.

Over the past 20 years he has gotten worse. In that time he's taken 200 lessons, possibly more. He's always looking for new information, so he never focuses on a similar source for his information. He hits balls five days a week, so it's not for lack of effort, but it is not focused effort, and it is a perfect example of how, if you're getting multiple sources of information, if you're practicing different things on different days of the week, there's no way for your brain to develop a pattern that's going to allow any kind of repetition.

So he's not only inconsistent, he's inconsistent hitting the ball left, then right, hitting it high, hitting it low—he's tried it all, but he's never tried the same thing long enough to develop any consistency.

Stick to one source of information, then repeat this information until you develop a solid brain-to- body connection that will govern your swing.

28. DON'T LET YOUR EGO INTERFERE

If you want to improve, know yourself and your abilities. There are players at every course, and they tend to be men, who overstate their abilities to themselves.

We have a foursome of men who have been successful in the business world and they have assumed that success in one part of one's life carries over. They are legitimate 10 to 15 handicappers, but fancy themselves somewhere between three and six.

I usually play with a members group on Sunday mornings, and when I'm with this foursome the scenario is always the same. One of them will be, say, 170 yards from the hole, uphill and into the wind, a shot for which I'll use a four or five iron.

He'll hit seven iron, wind up 35 yards short and say "I didn't get it all."

They conduct their entire golfing life denying their true abilities, and as a consequence they are always going to be disappointed.

There's nothing more important, if you really want to improve, then being honest with yourself.

29. "I MADE YOU ELEVEN"

He was an investment banker with a handicap around nine, and I was a 24-year-old fledgling professional, and when we got together on the tee for our opening session, he took an inordinate amount of time over his first ball—about 30 seconds. So I asked him what his swing thoughts were. "I have a 10-point checklist," he said, "three setup thoughts, five backswing and two thoughts for the downswing."

"I was a pretty good player at one point," I said, "and I've played with a lot of good players and teachers, and I've never seen anyone spend that much time thinking about what he was going to do, so if you're going to take any profit out of these lessons, its important that we limit our thinking to two pre-swing thoughts and the swing itself to one thought."

So on the next ball, instead of 30 seconds in his stance he took about 35 seconds.

"What happened? " I asked.

"I made your suggestion number 11," he said.

30. PLAY TO "YOUR" PAR

Par at most golf courses is 72, which in broad terms means if you are a scratch golfer, that is what your better scores should be. According to the United States Golf Association less than one per cent of male amateurs and less than one-tenth of one per cent of women amateurs are at this level or better.

So as a practical matter, par for you is most probably a higher number, and one way to improve your game is to plan your round based on that number. Once you can play consistently at that level, then you can lower the target number.

If your better scores average 85, your handicap is probably 12, so use 85 as your realistic par. Consider the first through 12th most difficult holes as having a par one stroke higher than the "regular" par, and plan accordingly (Practically all score cards indicate the relative difficulty of the holes).

For example: If the No. 1 handicap hole is a 460-yard par four, it doesn't make any difference if you're long enough or not long at all. If you're long enough, your handicap indicates that you're also crooked. If you play it with a three wood off the tee, then a five iron, in all probability you'll have an easy wedge left to the green, a reasonable chance at a five and even a four—and you'll rule out six and seven. Only play those shots you feel you have at least a 75 per cent chance of executing reasonably well.

If you're not long, rule out trying to jump on the tee shot for a few extra yards, and accept, from the start, the fact that you'll be hitting your third shot from the fairway.

There's no room on the scorecard for descriptive material—only numbers

31. THE RIGHT TEE

One of the two courses at our club is a former PGA Tour venue, and there were times when it included four of the most difficult holes the pros played all year. But the opening hole is short, only about 315 yards from the back, so people who aren't familiar with the course assume they're going to play the championship tees, thinking "Let's play where the pros played." Almost inevitably they walk off the 18th green with their heads down, their backs are stiff, and they didn't have an enjoyable experience.

Playing a course that is too difficult for you has a negative effect on your swing. You will be spending four hours trying to hit shots that you're not capable of hitting—fairway wood shots from downhill lies to elevated greens, for example. You're going to swing too hard, you're going to swing off balance, you're going to mishit the ball.

If the course you're playing is one with which you are not familiar, before you tee off look at the par fours on the score card and get an idea of their average length. Be realistic about how far you carry the ball with your tee shot, and know that in order to enjoy yourself, your second shots on the par fours, assuming you hit a good drive, should not be longer than 170 yards.

If all your second shots on the par fours will be from 190 to 230 yards or more, and you can't hit a tee shot that far, then you're certainly not going to be capable of hitting a shot of that length from a fairway lie.

So both from the enjoyment standpoint, and perhaps more important, from how this round is going to affect your swing on a long-term basis, play the course where you can hit shots you're capable of executing. That's going to help you swing on balance, develop a much better shot pattern, and have more fun.

Do not underestimate the importance of playing the "right" tees.

32. TAKE A TIP TO YOUR TEACHER

If you are a serious golfer, the amount of information "out there" is staggering. It's like being on the receiving end of an artillery barrage. You've got Golf Digest and Golf and other magazines, there is the Golf Channel, you have friends who consider themselves knowledgeable, and you have your teaching professional.

Nearly all of what you read, see and hear is correct—for someone, but not necessarily for you.

So what do you do with this overload of information? Discuss it with your teacher, who has outlined an improvement path for you:

Will it help me at this point in my development?

You have to find a way to filter this information so it doesn't become a negative.

For instance: "I've heard if your grip is lighter, it will help you create more club head speed."

Perhaps your teacher says that is contrary to what you're working on at the moment, or maybe it is some information you don't need at this point, because you're already doing this.

If you don't have a mentor, then write down the thoughts you've gathered from various places and then take a look at where you're at in your development. Remember, golf education is not a one-week process, it is a 30-year process.

But where you're at currently—can this particular information help you or hurt you?

Does it clarify things or does it confuse things?

Does it make you think too much, or does it make you think the right amount?

And if you decide that it is going to help you, and that it helps you think more efficiently, then by all means use it.

If not, just set it aside, because correct information out of sequence is incorrect information.

33. NOT SO HOT PEPPER

One of our members is a major rock band promoter and a few years ago, when the Red Hot Chili Peppers were in New York, he asked if I would play with Mike (Flea) Balzary, the Peppers' bass man. My son is a guitarist and a fan of the Peppers, so I enlisted him as Flea's caddy, and off we went.

Flea made about a 15 on the first hole, which is a short par four where bad players make a seven. On the second hole he whiffed a couple of times and then finally hit one off the tip of the club, and then I asked him how long he had been playing, and he said about a year.

"I live in Malibu," he said, and take lessons every couple of weeks when I have time, because of my career, " and I said "Would you mind my giving you a couple pieces of advice?"

"That's fine," he said.

"Well, first tell me what you're thinking about."

And typically, as a new golfer, he had a 10 to 15-point checklist to think about before each swing. Instead of all that, I gave him two setup keys and one swing key, and by the time we got to the back nine he actually made two pars, which on our course isn't easy.

When he was done, he said that was the best day he ever spent on a golf course. The story wasn't that I had any great wisdom, but what I did do was reduce his thought process, so he went from someone who was going to shoot almost 200 to someone who probably shot something near 120, and had a new perspective.

So if nothing else, you learn that the less you think, by definition, things will be better, and hopefully the things you are thinking about are correct.

But we enjoyed the day, and my son got to meet one of his idols and who now has become one of his mentors—in music, that is. Not golf.

34. PRACTICE, OR BEATING BALLS ?

We had a former tour player on our staff a few years ago, and one day, as I was headed for the lesson tee I saw him sitting at the back of the range. So I drove by and asked him what he was doing. It was a hot July day and there were 40 or 50 golfers swinging away, and puffs of smoke were rising from the dry ground, and he looked at me and said, "So many swings, so few hits."

It is so true: The number of range balls hit in vain is staggering. None of us is going to hit only good shots, but there are two main issues:

Most people are operating without a concept and without a plan. What they are doing, aside from possibly helping their tan, is a waste of time. When you go to the range you have to have a plan and it has to fit into your over-all concept.

For example: Let's say you're going to work on a backswing key and a downswing key. So roll out five balls and practice the backswing key with each of the five. Then do the same with the downswing key, and then move on to the next club.

Do not stand there with a seven iron and hit 60 balls just because you're not hitting the ball well. If you're not, try the "Back to Success" method:

If you mishit three shots in a row what you need to do is drop down two clubs. By doing this is you put less pressure on your swing and then when you've hit five good shots with the lower club you can advance to the longer one.

If you hit more than three bad shots in a row obviously something's going on in your swing and you need to gear down a little bit.

Gearing down can also be an effective practice system. In 1981 our Westchester Classic was the Tour event immediately after the U.S. Open, won that year by Australian David Graham. He was at the back of our range on the Tuesday of the Classic, with almost no one watching him, and he as hitting a driver, then a wedge, a driver, and then a wedge. When a friend of mine asked him why, Graham said "If I stood here and hit 40 consecutive drives, by the fifteenth one my tempo would be picking up through trying to hit the ball too hard and I'd lose my form. By hitting a driver and then going to a wedge it gives me a nice pattern."

Fast forward 30 years and my friend was in Palm Springs watching an LPGA event and who was doing the same thing? Annika Sorenstam.

Another way to make good use of your practice time is to "play" the golf course. You know your course, so take your 14 clubs and tee off on the first hole, figure out where the ball would land, and take whatever club would be appropriate for the next shot, and so on.

It's effective because it gives you visualization for your shots and you're hitting shots that you're going to hit on the course.

So have a plan when you go out there—what clubs are you going to hit, how many balls per club, stick with your plan. Whatever your swing keys are, stick with those, if you're going to "play the course" stick with that—and again, we're talking about practicing, not warming up.

Warming up is a separate issue—warming up is 20 balls before going to play, doing some stretching, But for practice, have a plan and stick to it. If you're hitting the ball poorly, you can change the plan for the next time, but at least give the plan a chance to work, don't just roll the balls out and start whacking them.

Try keeping a minute between balls. You have several minutes between balls on the course, so why speed things up on the range? Think about your next shot.

Practice is not usually transferable. You often hear "I hit the ball much better on the range than I do on the course." Why is that?

Much of this is because you're result-oriented on the course, and so you're projecting into the future and you get tight. Secondly, it is because your routine differs on the range. So whatever pre-shot routine you determine is yours, use it in both places: Hitting a 9-iron on the range should be no different than hitting a 9-iron on the course.

35. WHAT NEXT?

Your head is now filled with all sorts of information, and some of it will have a direct effect on your score.

So what's the next step?

Select the chapters that are most relevant to your particular problems and divide them into three categories:

- Most important
- Should be addressed
- Will get to when I have time.

Then focus on the items that are most important to you. Don't just put check marks in the book—write them down, as taking the time to put it all on paper will make the priorities more clear in your mind and be helpful in the long run.

36. ROCKEFELLER COUNTRY

Sleepy Hollow Country Club, about 25 miles due north of New York City on the east bank of the Hudson River, was founded in 1911, and at that time it had such illustrious names as Astor, Vanderbilt and Rockefeller on its board of directors. Its next-door neighbor is Kykuit, the 3,400-acre estate that is the home of the Rockefellers.

They have their own nine-hole course (with 18 tees) that winds between their houses, but they have always been Sleepy Hollow members and supporters, and I taught some of the family when I was at Sleepy, my last teaching job before becoming a head professional.

Nelson Rockefeller was just finishing his term as vice president in the Gerald Ford administration—this was 1976, and Jimmy Carter had become president—he was moving back to the estate, and I was asked to teach his two boys, Mark and Nelson Junior.

Nelson had hired his Secret Service contingent away from the Government and brought them to the estate, as there were a number of high-profile abductions going on at the time, and he felt more security is better, so he just moved his team in. I had to be interviewed by them and get a security clearance, which was somewhat unsettling for a 24-year-old, but I went on to develop a relationship with the family through the boys.

One day I got a call from David Rockefeller, Nelson's brother who was chairman of the Chase Manhattan Bank at the time, and he said he was planning on retiring and wanted to play more golf, and when could we start working.

So we did, and he came to the lesson tee with a set of rusted Spalding irons, and I gave him a few lessons with those and then I said "Mr. Rockefeller, you're not going to be able to improve with this equipment. Maybe we'll get you a set of Ping irons and some Ping woods and see how that helps your game."

This was in May, early in the season, and he thought about it for a moment, and then said "John, my birthday's in the fall, so what we'll do is my wife can get the irons for my birthday and my children will get together and buy the woods."

At that point I was making $125 a week and he was one of the world's wealthiest people—and I was worried about him getting new clubs.

As time went on we developed a great relationship, and eventually I became privy to one of his ambitions."You know, John," he said, "One of my goals is not only to play better, but I want to beat Bob Hope one time. Bob and I have been playing for years in Palm Springs.

"We're both getting older," he said, but I'm younger than he is and I should be able to play at his level at some point."

Six months after that I was in the shop one day and I got a call. Mr. Rockefeller was in Palm Springs and he said "I just wanted to let you know, I beat Bob Hope today. I shot 92 and he had 95."

III—PLAYING THE GAME

37. DIVIDE THE DAY

What it comes down to, after all the philosophizing and general good advice, is getting out there and playing, and avoiding those mental errors that held you back in the past.

First, realize the time spent on the course is only a third of it. Divide the day into three parts:

- Before
- During
- After

The "before" and "after" segments are applicable to players of all levels. The "during" section is also divided by three, for players with handicaps under 5, handicaps of 5 to 12, and handicaps of 13 or more.

38. BEFORE YOU PLAY

Getting ready takes time, a bit of preparation, a little bit of planning. Remember, failing to plan means planning to fail.

Once you know your tee time you can estimate how long it will take you to get to the course, how long it will take you to get to the range, how much time you want to spend on the range, how much time you want to spend on the putting green, and so when you get to the first tee you're not rushing and you haven't left anything out of your warm-up.

There will be days when you don't have time to do anything—you're at the office, you can just about get to the course, change your shoes and run to the first tee. If that's the case then skip the range and just do some light stretching on the first tee. There are some golf-specific stretches you can do to get your body as limber as possible.

Also, utilize the time spent driving to the course by doing your breathing exercise, which we will discuss later in the chapter entitled "Meet Doctor Bacci." That way you'll be able to maximize your opportunity for that day. But on a day when you do have time to prepare, you should get to the course at least an hour before your tee time.

And if you have a decent amount of distance to cover you want to make sure you're not driving at 90 miles an hour. All those things have an impact. I remember when I was a young professional living in Orlando and a friend of mine was caddying for Tom Kite. He was playing in the Citrus Open at Rio Pinar and my friend went to the hotel to meet Kite and Lee Trevino was there and he said "Why don't you come along with me?"—They were both from Texas—"Why don't you come along with me in my limo, we're going out to the course."

So Kite got in and there were Trevino and his caddy and my friend and Kite and there were about four other people in there and it was like a party for about 20 minutes...the screaming, the yelling, the limo driver, the whole thing...he said when Kite got to the range he was visibly shaken. The next day, he said Kite was one stroke off the lead and said "I'm going to drive myself," and my friend remembered that he was driving on the Interstate, and he was doing about 40 in a 60-mile zone, and my friend said "What are you doing, Tom?" and Kite said "I'm trying to get myself set for the day."

It's a simple story but it shows how you prepare yourself to play, and if you don't think that what you do prior to going to the course impacts how you play, you're mistaken. You may be lucky, and if you start playing well all the "other stuff" goes away, but if you start playing marginally or poorly, all the things that you did prior to, or that you carry with you to the first tee, will affect your play.

Each time you play, you have a special opportunity:

- To succeed (to play well)
- To identify areas in which you can improve
- To develop mental and emotional skills
- To improve and/or develop relationships

At the very least, don't turn this opportunity into a negative by leaving the course without having accomplished at least one of the above.

So now you've allowed enough time to get there, you go to the range,....always, always, start with little shots.. they don't have to be 15-yard shots, 30-40 yard shots are fine...hit six, eight, ten of those just get a feel of the ball on the clubface...to often people try a full swing even with a wedge and they mishit shots and so they start out with a negative image...hit some pitch shots, let your body start warming up, then hit maybe five balls with four different clubs...I don't think you need to hit more than 20 or 25 balls before a round.

Ideally, unless your game is really suffering, you're not working on more than one swing thought when you're warming up, what you're doing is warming up your body and getting yourself prepared to play. "Dance with the girl your brought," is applicable here, and if you're hitting a fade on the range, and that's what you feel, you probably need to play that fade on the course.

Every day, your body is different in some way. It's an amazing thing in golf, all the years I've been around it, people will be on the range and they'll have a swing thought, and they'll say "That's it, I'm going to use that forever, and I'm going to hit the ball well," and they come out the next day with the same swing thought and they're at about 60 per cent efficiency and they'll say "I'm terrible."

They're not terrible, their thoughts aren't terrible, it's just that their body is different. You need to recognize that some days you're looser than others, some days you're calmer. You need to recognize that although breathing can help you be a little more consistent with your level of anxiety, and remember that using the range before you play is basically just to warm up your body.

Then get yourself to the putting green. Work on short putts first, then try some lag putts, and then you're ready to go to the tee. Get yourself organized, make sure your cart or caddy is ready, and that's it. You're ready.

39. WHEN YOU'RE LATE

The last time you were in a gym it was to watch your kids play, your wife gave you an early-morning lecture about cleaning the basement, traffic held you up, and now it's 10 minutes to tee time. What do you do to get ready, aside from making resolutions about this never happening again: Do you head for the driving range, the putting green or just stretch?

First get the necessary details out of the way: Make sure the caddie master, or starter, or whoever is running the first tee, is aware you are there and your bag is where it should be.

Then stretch. Considering the amount of time you have available and the distance to the range, all you will gain by running over there with your driver and slashing at three balls is the likelihood of becoming even tighter.

Take two clubs—irons—and go off to the side, where you're out of the way, and do two simple stretches: The first one is to put the two clubs behind your back and hooked under your arms, and while in your stance and holding your lower body still, turn your upper body to the right, and hold that position for a count of five. Do this five times and then repeat, now turning your body to the left. This should help loosen your lower back.

Now take the same two clubs and hold them about waist high in both hands, and swing them back and forth slowly, just warming up. The weight of the two clubs will open up and warm up your upper back and shoulders.

Finally, take the two clubs in both hands—this is best with your two longest irons—and hold them at chest height, with your hands as far apart as possible, and one palm facing the sky and one facing the ground.

Now cross your arms so they form an "X." Do this several times, first one way and then the other, and hold for a few counts each time. This will stretch your shoulder muscles.

So in a just a few minutes you will have stretched your lower back, your upper back and your shoulders. Then I would use your last few minutes on the putting green, with a few two-footers first and then a few 10-footers, and next week, get there earlier. You can save more strokes by being on time.

40. THE FIRST TEE

Monique Thoresz, who has been one of the mainstays of our Westchester staff for several years now, knows that first-tee jitters can be a problem for even the best of players.

"No matter what they tell you," she says, "Everyone who plays golf is nervous, to a greater or lesser degree, on the first tee. The difference comes in how we handle it.

"Better players, more experienced players," she adds, "Use that nervousness as a welcoming feeling, 'a friend,' some call it, and they use it as a sign that they are ready. When they feel butterflies, or whatever their particular indicator is, that's a sign they're ready for competition, ready to do something special. Many of our better players think that if you're not feeling a little anxiety, something's wrong—you're not engaged.

"And if you're a beginner, or a high handicapper, no matter what you might think, everyone's not looking at you. The other players in your group are only worried about themselves. So don't worry about them.

"To the extent that you can," Monique says, "You want to be as relaxed as possible, and one way to do this is to focus on your breathing. Take deep breaths, 'belly' breaths, in and out of your abdomen, and let the air out very slowly. When we get nervous we don't breathe as much, the air's not going in and out of our abdomen, we get tight and as a consequence are physically incapable of swinging the club properly.

"Better players, low-handicap amateurs and professionals, may focus on something down the fairway. For higher handicappers, I think it is better to focus on your tempo, thinking perhaps, 'one, two,' with one being the backswing and two the through swing. Or think about making sure your alignment is correct, and then just swing freely."

41. DURING THE ROUND

LOW HANDICAPPERS (0-5)

- We tend to make the assumption that better players know everything, but there are a number of basics that even good players tend to forget. First, and this can be done before you get to the course, think about your opponent for the day.

Once you know your pairing, irrespective of whether you're playing at a private or a public course, you will probably know the player, and you probably have had some previous experience with him, so it is important that you get clear in your mind what to expect in terms of his personality and how you interact with him.

- Pace of play can be an issue—very often your opponent (or even your partner) will be someone who is slower or faster than your normal pace, so be prepared—not necessarily to play at their pace, but to be able to deal with it.
  Do this in advance, so you won't get out there and then be frustrated by this and have it impact your performance.
- Before you go to the tee identify your caddy. If you're playing at a private club you've probably had this caddy before, so get clear in your mind how he behaves. If you have issues, you want to deal with them before you go out. If he tends to be too talkative you may tell him I appreciate the input, but out here if I ask you for information give it to me, otherwise don't.

Ben Hogan was well known for wanting his caddy to do three things: Show up, keep up, and shut up. Maybe you need or want a lot of advice, maybe your caddy for the day is someone you trust and tend to lean on for advice. But make sure he knows what you want up front, so you don't have to deal with it on the course.

- Then you want to establish your pre-shot routine. Make sure you stay with your normal routine. If it's a slow round you don't want to be taking 10 practice swings if you usually take two. If it's a fast round you don't want to be pushed into not taking any.

- Get to your " ball area" as soon as you can because that gives you more control over your environment. That doesn't mean you want to go 50 yards in front of your fellow competitor, but you can find ways to move up when the opportunity presents itself.

- Recognize the day's ball-flight and body-movement patterns as soon as you can. Do this on the range first, seeing whether the ball has a tendency to go left to right or right to left, and whether you are particularly stiff or (hopefully) flexible. Remember, this is a warm-up, not a practice session and you're going to simplify matters by allowing for whatever your tendencies are at the moment. When you get to the golf course this may change—you become a little bit tighter, or looser, the ball may fly a little straighter or a little more curved.

  Just recognize it, allow for it, and don't try to fight it.

  This may change as the round goes on, but certainly, if you're hitting the ball left to right [for a right-handed player] you don't want to try and play a draw to a left-side pin for your first iron shot of the day. Recognize your situation.

- One of the important skills a low-handicap player can work on during the round is improving the ability to stay " in the present"—maintaining focus. This refers to our previous chapter on the skill of breathing, of being attentive to your breathing so you're not focused on your mechanics. More importantly, it will enable you to not focus on the results, either before or after, not being worried about the fact that's going to take even par to qualify, or that you hit a bad tee shot on the first hole and you're going to be one over after one. That shouldn't even be in your mindset.

  The ability to stay" in the present" is something you can practice during the course of the round, and you can develop your own method as to how to do that. The cliché that says you play one shot at a time is fine, but it has to be more concrete than that.

You have to have specific skills to know how to play one shot at a time, how to be in the present, how not to let your emotions overwhelm you, how not to project into the future, how not to look to the past. Proper breathing will help you do that.

- It is also useful for low-handicap players to look at the course in six-hole segments. Many people play a course in their mind before they actually play, maybe the night before, maybe as they are driving to the course. While you're doing this, look at it in segments. If you know the course then you know, more less, how you should play the first six, whether you should be even, or one, two or three over, and as you go along keep that in perspective. If you can do that, and if you double the first hole, you can maintain your confidence by knowing that you're still on target—or not that far off—for your first six-hole score.
So if you're two over for the first six even though you doubled the first you've obviously responded well to the pressure, but that's the whole purpose of developing six-hole segments.

LOW TO MID-HANDICAPPERS (6-12)

For these players a useful tactic is to concentrate on making your worst mistake into nothing more than a bogey. Obviously if you hit one out of bounds you can't control that, but if you've kept the ball in play, look to make no worse than a bogey after a bad shot.

- I've played a lot of rounds where I've made four, five, six bogeys and still shot even par. It's the double bogeys that will really kill you, both in terms of your score and in terms of your ability to see that you can turn the thing around with a birdie.
- So when you look at a bad shot: Think, how am I going to make a bogey out of this?
- Occasionally you're going to make a putt and save a par but you don't want to be putting yourself in a position where you're making two, three double bogeys in a round. If you're a low handicapper, it's going to be hard to break 75 if you have those doubles.

- Since you're going to be out there for four hours, keep some stats on an alternate score card while you're on the course. At a minimum, keep drives in the fairway, greens hit in regulation, up and downs for pitch shots and sand shots, and number of putts.

- If you want to do something more specific, up and downs inside 50 yards would be helpful, so when you sit down later, if you shot 84 and you normally shoot 76, you should analyze the round. You might think you hit the ball poorly when in fact you hit 14 greens but had 37 putts—but you got so frustrated with two tee shots that you think it was your driver. So you go running to the range and start fooling with your swing. Keeping statistics as you go can prevent this.

HIGHER HANDICAPPERS (13 AND OVER)

- Be realistic. The opening three holes should be used for setting the tone for the round, physically and psychologically, so take a high-percentage club to get it in the fairway off the first tee. You could go as low as a five wood, but a lot of players should hit three wood. I remember one winter where the course I worked at was very tight and I played a couple of rounds and then I said I'm going to play a three wood off the tee all winter, and I never saw the other side of 75. Played a course in Naples, Florida and never shot higher than 75, hitting a three wood off every tee.

  The great Australian Peter Thomson, four-time winner of the British Open, won at Saint Andrews one year when he never hit more than four wood off the tee. Tiger Woods won the British Open at Hoylake in 2006 and used his driver just once in four days.

- Recognize what you need to do to get the ball in the fairway.

  So let's assume you've an OK shot, an 80 per cent efficient shot, and you're down the fairway, and you've got 180 yards to the green, which is fairly well bunkered.

  As a middle-handicap player, the odds of you hitting a five wood or a hybrid for the second shot of the round to an elevated, bunkered green are probably one in five. So take a six iron and hit it to 40, 50 yards from the green.

You have a better chance to hit the ball in the middle of the club face, you're going to take some stress off yourself, and you're allowing your body to warm up. I know you've done your warm-up on the range, but the course is different than the range. The level of tension on the golf course is going to make your swing shorter for a period of time, and this condition could last two or three holes. So lay up short of the green, hit to area that's 40, 50 yards wide. If it gets narrow down near the green, then hit it to 70 yards.

- For your pitch shot, if your pin is in a difficult position near an edge, play to the wide part of the green. Use a little less-lofted club for your first pitch shot, so you might hit a pitching wedge instead of a sand wedge,. Again, the margin of error will be in your favor. You'll have to make a little shorter swing so you're more likely to make good contact with the ball, and if you leave yourself a 20-foot putt and make a bogey, that's a plus.

- The worst thing you can do is hit a poor tee shot, dribble your second shot, skull your third and end up with a triple bogey. Not only have you not learned anything about making good contact, but psychologically you're in a really bad place and you think this is terrible, I'm not going to play well today, versus the other way where you're OK, I'm in control, I'm not setting the world on fire, but I've got a little bit of a pattern going. Follow this strategy for at least two holes and possibly three.

- If you can do this you can develop good ball contact, your body's going to start warming up, and you might surprise yourself and make a par—you might be better than you think. In any case you're going to be no worse off.

- Divide the 18 holes into six three-hole segments. Many higher handicappers tend to get too far ahead of themselves, so limit your planning. Say OK, this is my three-hole group, and I should play these in four over par—that's your goal.

- You should have three-hole goals, and evaluate each segment at its' completion. Let's say you played the first three holes and you were two over instead of your "normal" four over. Obviously you're two strokes ahead of where you usually are, and this will allow you to play a little more aggressively going to the second three holes and the third three holes, and so forth.

- At the end of the day, you will be surprised at how well you've scored. Remember, there's no room on the card for descriptive material—only numbers.
- There will be days, however, when nothing works. That's life, and that's golf. If you let yourself be overwhelmed by the fact that you're seven over par after three holes and the day is essentially over, then you've forgotten some of the reasons for playing.
- No matter how badly you're playing, get something out of every round. If you're hitting the ball poorly, focus on your putting. If your hitting the ball well and putting poorly, say to yourself "I can't seem to get my stroke going, so I want to make sure to focus on my course management, or my ball striking, or I want to make sure that my tee shots are high percentage."

You should always walk off the 18th green better for having been out there, and even if all these things we've discussed fail, at least you've been out in a beautiful environment, possibly with some good friends, and that can't be bad.

There's always tomorrow.

42. AFTERWARDS

A word of caution: If you don't stretch before going in for lunch your body will stiffen, and if you want to get any real benefit out of your post-round practice, you should go through your entire stretching routine before starting to hit balls.

It's that important. Ten minutes will do it, and this will also help your body long term

After lunch, go to the range for a good 30-minute practice session—maximum 40 balls, maximum 10 balls per club, four to six clubs, start with your lower clubs and work on your swing mechanics.

Work on whatever is important to you at this time. Be target-oriented, so you're not just whacking balls. Pick out a specific distance and a target—if you're hitting nine iron and your nine-iron distance is 120 yards, pick a target at that distance, and if you don't have good targets on your range pick a general area, but be specific, even to the point that you can visualize a shot of that length on your course.

If you normally have a nine-iron to the 15th green, then say OK, I'm going to hit 10 nine-irons to the 15th green, and visualize it. That will help you in your ability to visualize shots. And go through your full routine: Take a practice swing if you normally take one, if you're going to work on taking a deep cleansing breath before you set up to the ball go ahead and do that, but don't rush—hit fewer balls, but do the proper routine and have a good target.

In a good practice session you won't hit more than one ball per minute, and you will take anywhere from two to four practice swings before each ball. That's practice, as opposed to beating balls.

Be aware of the fact that most range balls do not carry as far as the ones you've used on the course. They've been hit hundreds of times and are worn out, so concentrate on direction and trajectory, and on getting the feeling of making good contact. After a good practice session you can put your clubs away and go home and feel better, even if you played poorly. I've done my stretching and now I've got a little plan that I can work on.

And even if your practice didn't go well, at least you've had some time to focus on the mechanics you're working on and then you can debrief with your pro or yourself and look forward to the next day. It is important not to leave the course with a defeatist attitude—because that is the mindset you'll carry to the course tomorrow.

43. IS THE YARDAGE CORRECT?

So here you are on the tee of a par three listed on the card at 150 yards. You take your 150-yard club, hit it well—and are 20 yards short.

How does this happen? Why was the hole playing 170 yards?

The basic reason for the variance is what we can call "The Rule of Six," which most superintendents use to maintain the condition of the course, the integrity of the course's total yardage, and of the challenge it should present.

By this we mean that, generally speaking, six holes will have easy pin placements, six will be medium, and six will be difficult. At the same time six will be located in the back portion of the greens, six will be in the middle and six will be in front. The same exercise will take place on the teeing grounds—six front, six middle and six back—for each set of tees.

So before you step up to hit your shot, locate the permanent distance marker that is usually embedded at the side of the teeing ground, and walk off the distance to today's tee. Some tees can be 40 yards in depth, and some greens can be 40 yards deep.

If it is uphill and into the wind, that 150-yard hole can be playing 190 yards. Conversely, downhill, front tee, downwind, front pin, it could be playing 120 yards.

Some other thoughts about yardage in general:

- The worse the lie, the more it will affect a long shot.
- Uphill lies mean the shot will be longer, but the reverse is not necessarily true. Downhill lies can also play longer, probably because shots of this type usually have overspin.
- If the ball is below your feet the shot will most likely fade and it won't go as far. If it is above your feet, you can expect it to go farther than usual.
- Wind almost always hurts more than it helps. A crosswind against your natural shot (left to right or right to left) will tend to knock the ball down, a crosswind with your natural shot will tend to help it. Even straight downwind, if your shot is too high, the wind will knock it down.

- Weather: if the day is damp or very cloudy, the heavy air will have a negative effect on distance. The same when it is chilly, or it is early in the morning and the ball has been sitting in damp grass.
- Golf balls are sensitive to temperature, so when you are playing in cold weather make sure the balls you use were inside last night, not sitting in your bag in the trunk of a car. Rotate two or three balls while playing and keep the ones not in play in your pocket where they can warm up. You might note that the Rules of Golf allow the use of a hand warmer for you, but not for the golf balls.
- Footing—if the ground is soft your stance will not be solid and your shot will not travel as far as it would from a "normal" lie.

44. HOW FAR DO YOU REALLY HIT IT?

The most obvious way is to use a launch monitor, but before we get to that, let's think about why we want to know this:

It not so you can brag in the locker room. You should know this so that you can plan your strategy, and the distance you carry your driver may well turn out to be the least important piece of information you have. What you need to know is the carry distance of every club in your bag.

Many clubs have launch monitors and so do the fitting departments of many major golf retailers. If you don't have access to one, a portable range finder, for sale nationwide, will do almost as well.

Assuming you don't have access to either one, be careful of using driving-range distances as your standard. You're usually hitting off a mat to a downhill target area, and you are hitting balls that lost their dimples (and their distance) long ago. Sometimes the targets are not measured correctly.

As an alternative, pick four or five spots where it is fairly level, or even slightly uphill, on the course you play regularly (so you won't get a lot of bounce and run). Then pace off the distance from some fairway marker or sprinkler head to the center of the green. Do this after you've hit a shot—let's say you've just hit a seven iron, and you hit it particularly well, and you're in the middle of the green.

Do this on four or five holes with shots of different lengths and you should be able to develop a fairly realistic understanding. You don't want to measure a shot that bounces off hardpan and carries another 30 yards and think that's how far you hit it.

I'm referring to landing a ball on a green and having it come to rest within 15 feet of where it first hit. And if you do this, you should be able to have a realistic assessment of your length with various clubs. Do this in calm conditions, and definitely not downwind.

Can you get better? Sure you can, and then you can re-measure. But if you're standing over a shot of 150 yards and you once hit a seven iron that far but your average shot of that length is a five iron, if you take the seven you're going to try too hard and hurt your swing pattern.

So use the golf course, use a flat area, a slightly elevated green if possible, and walk it off.

Don't forget: The thing that should concern you after 18 holes is your score, not how far you hit that six iron on the twelfth.

45. MAKING IT LONGER

A few years ago we were considering lengthening our West Course, so I met with the PGA Tour's architects. Our sixth hole is a dogleg right par four that presently plays at about 465 yards from the tips and we wanted to get it up to 490 or 500 if we could.

So we went out to look at some areas where another tee might be placed, and we located one—just a turf area with a little bit of a downslope, and also a little gravelly.

While we were standing there Vijay Singh, Tom Pernice and Scott Hend, a long hitter from Australia, were coming off the fifth green. So we asked them if they would mind hitting from this spot so we could get an idea of how the corner would play from here. At this time Vijay was the number one player in the world.

He said "I'll do it for you," and he plugged a tee into the ground, complete with a downhill lie in the questionable area, and wiggled his feet into position. We have a tree on the corner of the dogleg that from this spot was probably 270 yards distant. It is roughly 70 feet tall, meaning it would take about a 320-yard shot to clear it.

He made as easy a backswing as you can imagine and flew it right over the corner, and then I realized that wherever we put the tee, we weren't going to be able to make it into a long par four for these guys.

It also gives you a look at the natural talent out on the tour, the ability to hit out of almost any position, and also a look at little bit of their ego, that they'd be willing to take a challenge. Then Hend said "I'll give it a go," and he stepped up and hit it over the tree.

I looked at Pernice, who is a medium-length hitter, and he shook his head.

"You've got to be kidding, "he said.

46. YOUR PRE-SHOT ROUTINE

Harvey Lannak is our head professional (I'm called the director) and a winner of the Metropolitan PGA Section's Teacher of the Year Award, which should give you some idea of the talent level of our instructional staff. One important point Harvey makes involves keeping to a consistent pre-shot routine. "This is one of the factors that separates good players from the rest," he says. "All the good players I've seen and worked with over the years have developed a precise pre-shot routine," he adds.

"It is something they practice, just as they practice hitting balls, putting, bunker shots, they practice their pre-shot routine," he explains. "And when you're under the gun, it can be a great security blanket. When you're in a pressure situation you can call on your routine, you get into your routine, and it can deflect some of the things that might interfere with your concentration.

"Good routines have some similarities. You'll almost always see the player aim the clubface first. He may trigger the routine, for example, by refastening the Velcro on his glove, then walk up to the ball from behind, aim the face, put his back foot in position, put his front foot in position, establish his distance from the ball and the ball placement (front, back or middle), and he'll do that with every club, every time.

"He even does the same thing on the range during practice.

"I've seen Billy Casper, the winner of two U.S. Opens, interrupt his routine when something happened to affect it," Harvey says. "Billy's routine was quick—he made his decisions and moved quickly, but if something stopped him in the middle, it would be like an aborted takeoff. He'd go back and start over, from the beginning."

47. COOPER AND CRENSHAW

The great Harry Cooper, a member of the Golf Hall of Fame, a winner of the Vardon Trophy and 31 professional tournaments, graced our Westchester lesson tee for almost 23 years, from the time he retired as a full-time club professional until his passing at the age of 96 in 2000.

Harry would be there most every morning with a line of supplicants waiting to hear his words of wisdom, and working next to him was an education. The esteem in which we all held him was perhaps best demonstrated by Ben Crenshaw in 1995, the year he won his second Masters. Ben was due at Westchester a month or two after Augusta, and before he arrived he called and asked if I could arrange dinner for the three of us. Ben is a student of golf history, and Harry was one of the first members of the Texas Golf Hall of Fame.

The Tuesday before that year's Westchester Classic saw the newly crowned Masters champion spend three hours soaking up the golfing lore of his home state from a man who never won the Masters, but was golf royalty nevertheless. Ben hardly said a word. At the end of the evening I asked Ben one question about his Masters victory: "How many three-putts did you have?"

"None," he said. Seventy-two holes at Augusta without a three-putt, and so self-effacing he never mentioned it.

Harry and his wife Emma were childless, so when he left us the direct line back to the very first full-time professional ended. Alan Robertson of St. Andrews is considered the first, back in the mid-1800's. Old Tom Morris was Robertson's apprentice and successor, and Sid Cooper, Harry's father, apprenticed under Morris.

In addition to his 31 wins he was second 37 times and added 25 thirds. His parents moved to Texas before World War I, and Harry's career started there, winning the Texas Open in 1923 at the age of 19. He won the Los Angeles Open twice, and when he took the Vardon Trophy in 1937 he won eight of the 14 events that made up what was then considered the Tour.

He lost the U.S. Open in a playoff in 1927, and was runner-up again in 1936. He was runner-up in the Masters twice, in 1936 and 1938.

He hardly ever spoke about it, but when he did, he almost always finished by saying he felt his career had been a failure.

Harry had high standards.

48. MIDDLE OF THE GREEN

Even if you are a scratch or low single-digit player, the conservative approach on shots to the green is almost always better. It might not provide birdie opportunities, but there will be holes later in the round where you can be aggressive. For now, a 30-foot putt is better than a bunker shot. There are exceptions of course, in certain match-play situations for example, or when getting it close on the last hole could mean winning a tournament.

If you're a left-to-right player, as are the majority of right-handed golfers, and the hole is located on the left side of the green, you basically have the middle-left and the entire right side of the green as a target. So your aiming point is not going to be outside the green and hoping the ball is just going to feather in to the flag. You want to aim at the flag, knowing that your left-to-right flight will give you possibly 20 yards of green to work with, rather than aiming at the left edge of the green and having only 10 or 15 feet as your margin for error.

Conversely, if you're a right to left player and the pin is on the right-hand side, then you don't want to start it at the right edge of the greenside bunker that is most likely close to the hole. Aim at the flag, and accept the fact that you've got the biggest area of the green to work with, from the flag to the left edge of the green.

Give yourself the widest possible margin for error. This will take pressure off your game.

The same applies to tee shots. Develop a swing pattern so that if you miss the shot, you can depend on the direction it will take—it is either going to go left or right. And since most right-handed players tend to miss to the right, obviously what you want to do is favor the left side of the fairway. That will give you the entire width of the fairway to use. You don't want to be aiming at the center. If you do, you'll be losing 10 to 25 yards of space by not aiming to the left.

If you happen to be hitting it fairly straight, then you'll have to decide which side you want to favor depending on your second-shot approach to the green. But in almost every case you should eliminate one side of the fairway, as that will allow you to swing with more confidence.

49. WHERE TO TAKE YOUR GRIP

This may seem like an oversimplification, but it is not.

I'm not telling you *how* to grip the club—that is up to your teacher—but *where* you should put your hands on it. If you watch most good players you will see they put their target hand—for right-handed players it is their left hand—on the club when their arm is hanging by your side.

The reason for this is that you should take hold of the grip when your arm and shoulder are in their most natural condition and are fully relaxed. Grip the club with your target hand, then swing the club in front of you, about belt high.

Now place your other hand on the grip, and you will see if the face of the club is square to the intended line of play. Now you can lower it to the ground and you're ready to go.

The idea of having the club at your side while you put your target hand on is essential to making sure you have both the proper grip and also that your arm is in a relaxed condition and your shoulder is not unnaturally stressed, which happens often when you take your grip with the club directly in front of you.

Most people take their grip with the club in front of them. When you move your arm in front, both your hand (and the arm to which it is attached, obviously) tend to rotate open. That's one of the reasons they are physically stressed before they even start to swing. .

50. "GIMMES"

This is not to belabor the obvious—that the game calls for all putts to be holed, unless conceded in match play. It is to point out that "gimmes" are not only a negative influence on your game, but can also affect formal competitions weeks and months down the road.

In stroke play the ball has to be holed, period. What concerns us here is the friendly match in which both of you are knocking away two-footers, recording scores as if they were holed, and therefore posting scores that are optimistic at best, and serve to artificially lower your handicap.

You are going to need to make that two-footer at some point in the future, and your lack of game experience with that little dear can only work against you. And your friend, who because of your generosity is now an 8 instead of a 9, will be playing in next month's member-guest at Happy Hollow and will embarrass his host—and himself—because he can't play to his number.

51. FAIRWAY BUNKERS

Your tee shot rolled into that bunker on the right side of the fairway and now you've got anywhere from, let's say, 140 to 250 yards to the green.

First priority: Get Out.

At least 50 per cent of the time I see players take a club that doesn't have enough loft, they hit the lip of the bunker and if they're lucky the ball pops out maybe 10 feet and they've lost anywhere from 60 to possibly 120 yards. In selecting the correct club, give yourself at least a one-club margin for error. So if you think it's a seven there's no harm in taking an eight, unless you think you can reach the green—comfortably—with the seven.

If you're good enough—based on your talent—then go with the longer club, but the margin for error should always be on your side.

Once you've got the club, take your grip. Many players secure themselves in position by working their feet into the sand and then taking their grip. I wouldn't do anything special with the grip, but it is important that you grip before you take your stance.

Play the ball a little more centered than you would on the fairway, so if you're using an eight iron and you normally play it a little forward of center, play it in the center of your stance, because the club must hit the ball before the sand. If you catch sand first you are going to lose anywhere from 30 to 60 per cent—if not more—of your effective hit.

The principal error most people make in fairway bunkers is losing their balance. It is better to hit an 80 per cent shot than a 10 per cent shot, so swing at about 70 per cent of normal speed to make sure you maintain good balance and make a clean strike.

Ball first, then sand.

If you can get the ball out cleanly, and you have a chance to knock the next one on you'll have a putt for a par and at worst a bogey. So be realistic in terms of club selection, move the ball back, and swing in balance.

52. PLAYING IN THE WIND

I remember Gene Littler one year at the Masters when the wind was blowing, saying "When it's breezy I swing it easy."

You might think just the opposite, that you would have to swing harder on a windy day because the wind affects the flight of the ball, but his point was that the more on balance you are, the more likely you are to hit the ball in the middle of the club face, and the more you hit it in the middle of the face the better the compression and the straighter and better the shot.

If you're playing in really windy conditions there are two basics:

- Widen your stance for increased stability.
- Play the ball just a little farther back in your stance, even with the driver. That will help you catch the ball on your downswing, so you'll trap the ball and give it a little lower flight, because you don't want it ballooning

Be careful not to play it too far back, because if you do you will create extra backspin and more lift—and more unwanted height.

If your normal six iron flies 150 yards and you're playing into a wind, instead of hitting a five iron you might consider choking down on a four iron and swinging easy, because when you swing easy you are going to use your hands less. When your hands are not as involved you get less spin, less lift, and the wind won't affect the shot as much.

So try dropping down two clubs, swinging easy, and playing the ball back. This will give you a lower ball flight and less spin, so you'll have more control. The main thing is to keep your balance so you'll have good center-face contact.

I would not practice a lot in heavy winds because you're going to have to develop a lot of compensating movements with your hands that are going to last a few weeks. Windy days are challenging, but they are part of the game. Playing on a windy day on a links course, maybe you're not going to shoot your best score, but playing through the elements is part of the challenge, so embrace it, don't complain about it.

53. PLAYING IN THE RAIN

If you live where you have a short season or if you're playing in a tournament, sometimes you've got to get out there regardless of the weather. And if you do, preparation can be everything if it's raining. If it's a cool rain it will be like playing in the cold—you want to make sure you have sufficient layers so your body doesn't get cold. There's nothing more damaging to your swing than to have your body cold internally and expect it to rotate properly, or if your hands get so cold they have trouble feeling the grip. Warmth is very important on a rainy day.

Basic things: Hopefully you have shoes that are waterproof, although most of them now on the market have at least a one-year guarantee. It wouldn't be a bad idea to carry an extra pair of socks because even though your shoes are waterproof sometimes the rain can get to your socks. Wet feet are second only to wet grips.

Rain suits are, or should be, a given. There are non-Gore Tex rain suits for around $200, but if you're going to play at lot in bad weather, spending $300-$400 on a rain suit is a good investment. You can also use it in cold weather, because a good rain suit is going to protect you against other elements as well.

A hat: If you wear glasses you want to make sure you have a wide-enough brim so that you don't have water dripping on your lenses.

Gloves: There are gloves designed specifically for playing in wet weather. If you can't find them, a simple pair of cotton dress gloves will help. They should be soaking wet for maximum adhesion.

Keeping your grips dry is paramount, and one thing you see a lot of tour players do is hang at least one and preferably two towels under the struts of your umbrella, because then when you take a club you can dry off the grip as well as drying your hands. Cord grips tend to be better in the rain than grips made of other materials.

If you're going to be riding in a cart, make sure you have enough towels in the cart to dry off the seat, even if you're wearing a rain suit. Anything that's going to get you physically prepared to play in the rain will help you to maximize the opportunity

54. AFTER A BAD ONE

"The most important thing after I've hit a bad shot," Monique Thoresz points out, "Is not that I know I have the skill to hit the next shot well, it's that I prepare myself mentally to hit the next one well.

"Golfers at all levels, even beginners, have to do the same thing. Put the bad news behind you and concentrate on what's next. "

55. A NEW PLATEAU

It's only a game.

But the first time you break 100, or 90, or 80, that's a big day in your golfing life, and you're entitled to a little celebration.

If you've played at all, you know the difference.

It is more than just one shot.

If it was the first time you broke 100, you are now in the land of double-digit golfers, previously *Terra Incognita*.

How did you get there? In all probability it was not by doing anything much different, it was most likely by making fewer mistakes and sinking a few more putts.

Think about that.

You'll be surprised at how much you can lower your scores just by the avoidance of mistakes and by putting better. You'll have to become a better course manager and ball striker if you want to continue your improvement past a certain level, but in the meantime better putting can do wonders for you.

56. THE CHAIRMAN

When I was at Sleepy Hollow we had some Japanese members, of whom it was said they were the most powerful Japanese businessmen in America. One of them was Akio Morita, the chairman of the board of the Sony Corporation.

He signed up for a lesson with me one day and I, in my youthful ignorance, had no idea who he was. About halfway through the lesson I gave him some drills to do at home or in the office. "You're a businessman and you obviously spend much of your time in your office," I said, "do you have room and time to swing?"

And he nodded and smiled and said "Yes, I have space."

And I said "I'm thinking about a lot of space, so you can swing a golf club."

And he nodded and smiled and said "Plenty of space."

And I said "Do you have time?" and he couldn't take it any more, and finally he said "John, chairman of the board, Sony."

About three nights later I was in a grocery store and at the checkout counter, there was the newest edition of People Magazine with his photo on the cover.

57. COMPETITIVE GOLF: IT'S DIFFERENT

When the PGA Tour comes to the New York metropolitan area each year, one or two of our local club pros manage to qualify. These are veterans, capable of playing in the 60's on difficult courses. Then the first round of the tournament comes and they shoot anywhere from 76 to the low 80's, do the same on Friday and are gone.

When I ask them why the difference in performance, they say "I was out of my element." The golf course was the same, but there were crowds, grandstands, television broadcast booths and advertising signs. They felt out of their element, and as a consequence they lost their focus.

When you are playing in a formal competition, especially at a course other than your home club, it is most important to be comfortable with this new situation, and the only way you're going to do that is by exposing yourself to it at lower levels. First of all, you need to know that if you're going to play competitive golf, even at a club level, you've got to play in some smaller club tournaments. You can't just jump into the club championship. Play in the team match play, or in the member-member, whatever it is—but play in the type competition you are going to play when you move up.

A lot of amateurs are usually playing a better-ball of two against another twosome, or singles match play, and then they enter something like the Westchester Amateur, which has a stroke-play qualifying round. Now they have to putt out 18 times and post a score and the results are usually much different than what their handicap indicates. So prepare for that—play some medal rounds where you have to putt everything in the hole and you'll be amazed, psychologically, how different that is if you haven't been doing it.

So let's assume you've played in a few "outside" tournaments and you're at least familiar with the surroundings. You know what it is to go up to a strange club and have somebody take your bag, going to a registration desk—simple procedural things, but you have to get used to them.

Then recognize that you are going to be anxious, and accept it. To expect that everything's the same and everybody's just out to have fun is not accurate. You are denying reality. You're going to be under your own self-imposed pressure. And remember, other people don't care what you shoot, certainly not the people you're playing with. They are golfing their ball and if they are good, you are barely in their line of vision. Some friends who read the local paper might see your name, but that's not all that we make it out to be.

So you have to decide in advance what your goals are. If your goal is to qualify, then you want to prepare, get your game ready, get yourself physically ready, do all the preparation you need to do and then play, knowing you're going to be anxious, accepting that pressure, not trying to deny or reduce the pressure a little bit when you try to say everything's fine and all of a sudden the pressure hits you like a ton of bricks. That's no good.

So expect that you're going to be anxious. This is where breathing can help you, to reduce your physiological tension. Don't try to behave any differently than you normally do. If you're a quiet person, be quiet, if you're a loquacious person be talkative. Don't change too much, because if you do you're going to be out of your own personal element as well..

Be aware of the fact that many people give up too early in the round. If you make bogeys on the first two holes, keep playing. There are so many examples of people who've played well over the last four or five holes to make the cut or to qualify, as compared to those who finished double-bogey, double-bogey to miss.

If you're going into a competition realize, up front, that funny things happen on a golf course. And remember, whatever else happens, every time you set foot on a golf course it is an opportunity to learn.

QUALIFYING

The more seasoned players have a number in the back of their minds. They know just about what score it will take to get into the match-play field of 16, or 32 or 64. If you don't, you can ask before you play. Ask one of the veteran officials, or someone else who knows, what scores typically get in, so you don't have to think even par is a must.

And finally, for competition versus fun golf, you should develop a "go-to" swing, one for when you're under the gun and anxious. Most tournament players have one—it could be a ball flight, left to right or right to left. Tiger Woods has his "stinger" swing, and it is not only to keep the ball under the wind, it is also to keep the ball in play. That's his go-to swing.

So develop something that will not travel quite as far, but can be counted on to stay out of the water and in bounds.

58. ADVICE FROM TOMMY

In the winter of 1973 I was a young assistant at Royal Poinciana in Naples, Florida, making $80 a week and working about 40 hours a week so my gross pay was $2 an hour, and when I had the opportunity to play in a tournament, dreams of major money were dancing in my head.

It was the Pabst Blue Ribbon Tournament, a 36-hole event at Fort Myers Country Club, a public course about 40 miles north of Naples. I happened to play well in the first round, shot 70, and so I was in the next to last group off the tee on the second day.

My pairing was with Tommy Bolt, the 1958 U.S. Open champion, member of two Ryder Cup teams and more famous, unfortunately, for his temper and his habit of throwing clubs. Bolt had one of the best swings in all of golf, and he had been my number one or two swing idols when I was a kid. I had the opportunity to watch him play in Hartford and at Westchester, and so I was really excited, both for the opportunity to play with one of the great swings of all time, and also for the opportunity to win, which paid $1,500—equivalent to about four months' work.

We had a one o'clock tee time and I got to the club at 8:30, which was about three and a half hours too early for a warm-up. So I hit balls and stopped, hit balls and stopped, about three or four times, trying to make sure I was ready.

I got to the tee at about a quarter to one, the preceding group had gone off, they made the first call for our pairing and there was no Tommy Bolt to be seen. There was a small parking lot and it was obvious that if he was on the grounds we would have seen him.

Then all of a sudden this Rolls-Royce appeared at the entrance to the course, which was parallel to the first hole, drove through the rough and pulled up next to the tee. A young blonde girl got out, popped the trunk and out came the clubs, then out stepped Tommy Bolt, complete with silver hair and wearing a windbreaker.

His clubs went to his cart and mine were on my cart. He didn't bother to introduce himself to me, the starter gave him my card and I had his, and I got up there on the first tee and hit some kind of a hook after about 10 practice swings. Bolt stepped up, with not even a practice swing, just a couple of waggles, and hit it about 260 down the middle, which in 1973 was a pretty long poke, especially for someone in his late 50's.

So we played along, and somewhere on the back nine I was about seven over par and not only were my chances of winning long gone, so was the opportunity of maybe making three or four hundred dollars and I was pretty upset with myself. There were canals along many of the holes, and I hit snap hook into one of them, and took my driver and slammed it down and it bounced back and hit me in the shoulder.

At this point Bolt walked over to me, and I thought he might say something about my grip, or my stance—something that might help me in the future.

"Son, I need to tell you something," he said. "When you're going to throw a club, throw them toe down—then they don't bounce back."

59. MATCH PLAY and STROKE PLAY

Tommy Murphy was the head professional at Sleepy Hollow when I was a young assistant there in the 1970's, and he had worked for Jack Grout at Scioto in Columbus, Ohio, in the late 1950's when Jack Nicklaus was growing up there. Grout was close to Texas legend Jack Burke Senior and Burke would send one or two young assistants up to work at Scioto every season, and one of their jobs was to play with the members.

Murph remembered this young guy with the red convertible and Texas plates who came in from playing with some members one day and Grout asked him "How'd you do?" and he said "I had 16 pars and two X's," and Grout said "You can pack your clubs now and go home to Texas. On my staff, you don't make X's."

The point is, of course, you can make 16 pars and shoot 80—you didn't shoot 72. So you need to understand that. Most amateurs aren't used to putting out, and they say "Just give me a six," when it might have been an eight or a nine. So when you're switching from match play to stroke play learn how to putt out, which may sound like a simple thing but isn't.

Corollary to that is learning how to make a bogey instead of a double bogey. Learn to make good decisions when you're playing stroke play. If you've hit a bad tee shot, start thinking how to make bogey rather than attempting some "hero" shot that like as not will lead to a double or worse.

Match play, obviously, is a different game and again, a lot of golfers play match play, but they don't play it wisely. Typically you don't have to play great to win matches, what you have to do is avoid making a lot of big scores. Consistency will wear down your opponent.

Even if you're just making bogeys (or pars if you are an ultra-low handicapper), keep the ball in the fairway, then hit the ball to the apron and chip up. This will wear down your opponent, because when he gets the feeling that you're a steady golfer, it tends to break his spirit. There may be a time when, say, you'll be three down with five to go and you'll have to be more aggressive with your game, aggressive with your putting, whatever it might be. But that's then, not at the start.

You should also recognize the state of your opponent's game. You can pick up on that fairly early. If he's having a great day you're going to have to play really well, but if he's not having a great day don't put yourself in a position where you're playing down to his level.

That happens surprisingly often in match play, where people play "down" to their competition. You want to play a steady game.

Let's say you hit a good drive on the first hole and your opponent has a terrible drive, and then dribbles his second shot and you're standing there with 160 yards to the flag and you have a clear plan of what your swing thought should be, and all of a sudden you say "Maybe I'll just hit down short of the green because he might not get on in three," and you start co-opting your swing thoughts and you start co-opting your original plan of how you feel. You want to stay in a good pattern, because it's so easy to let it start slipping away.

If you're opponent is playing poorly, don't play differently from how you feel. If you're not feeling great and you want to play conservatively that's one thing, but if you're hitting the ball well you want to stay with it. I'm not big on trying to back down too much—it affects your swing pattern, which is hard to recapture after it starts slipping away.

60. WHY YOU SHOULD KNOW THE RULES

Golf has a long tradition of honesty and integrity, one that separates it from practically every other game. It has 34 rules, and if you're a golfer you play by these. If you don't—and there is no golf policeman standing over you—you are merely someone who plays at golf, as opposed to being a golfer. If you decide to ignore the rules in certain situations, in the end you're only cheating yourself.

If you are playing in a tournament, you have two responsibilities—to yourself, and to everyone else in the field. In any given round things will happen that can affect your ability to score. It could be relief from a cart path, it could be an unplayable lie, it could be a hazard rule, it could be when you address the ball on a putting green on a windy day. For example, if you haven't grounded your putter and the ball moves and your opponent/ fellow competitor says "play the ball where it lies and it's a one-stroke penalty," you need to know the rules.

The rule book can be fairly complex, but I would certainly read through it at least once to get a general understanding. But become really familiar with the index, and learn how to find things, because most people take so much time to find the applicable rule that they get flustered and lose their focus and eventually the match. So learn the index.

As far as match play is concerned, knowing the rules is important because your opponent can call penalties on you that aren't so. I've seen people misunderstand the rules and say "I guess you win the hole." If you give up the hole you can't reclaim it later just because you failed to understand something. Once you tee off on the next hole it's a moot point.

Again, there are three reasons:

- Upholding the integrity of the game.
- In stroke play knowing the rules can help your score.
- In match play making sure you have a fair chance.

61. HANDICAPS AND INDEXES

Handicaps have been a part of golf almost since the game began, as these are the devices used to—theoretically at least—allow players of different abilities to compete on a level basis. For match-play (hole-by-hole) competitions, the system is simple:

If your handicap is eight and your opponent's is 14, he will be given a one-shot advantage on the six most difficult holes. Check a scorecard and you will see the holes are ranked for their degree of difficulty, with the odd-numbered ones on the front nine and the even-numbered on the back. The reason for the even-odd split is that in the case of this match, for example, the higher handicapper will get three shots on the front side and three on the back.

The handicap itself is not an average of all of your rounds. It is a number designed to reflect your peak performance, and although the exact formula is somewhat complicated, it is based on 96 per cent of your best 10 scores of your last 20 rounds. For a more detailed explanation, go to the U.S. Golf Association's website, USGA.org. It will also explain slope rating, which has to do with course rating, which leads us to index. In today's world, your index number is what you carry from one golf course to another, and use to check against the local slope rating to find what your handicap will be at this course.

Fortunately, GHIN (the Golf Handicap and Information Network) does all the calculating for you. All you have to do is plug in your scores.

There are several organizations that will calculate your handicap for you, with the USGA's GHIN system being the most popular (roughly two millions users). Almost every municipal or daily-fee course has a place where you can sign up to get a handicap, and if the one in your neighborhood doesn't, then go to the USGA website.

62. MORE ON PRACTICING

When you dump your bag of balls on the practice tee, it is a good idea to keep the balls behind you, so you don't start raking them over one after another and hitting them in rapid-fire fashion. If the big pile is behind you, you at least have to get up out of your stance and think a bit before taking the next one.

Divide the big pile into little groups of five balls, and put one of these piles facing you. Then work on a specific move with this group of five, then bring up another five balls, and work on another move, and go to the next club

Concentrating on the five balls you have put there for one specific practice move will help to keep your focus. And I don't believe you should hit more than 10 balls with any one club before moving to the next one, and limiting this to five is better.

63. MAKING DECISIONS

One mistake that some amateurs make—and the higher the handicap the more pronounced this becomes—is taking too long to make a decision, and too short a time to execute it.

A good player does a lot of preparation while the others in his group are playing their shots. He'll examine the line of a putt, or decide on which club to hit, before it is his turn to play. As a result he has the time to make his swing in a deliberate manner.

Many amateurs act as spectators until it is their turn, and then they rush up to hit their shot because they're worried about being out of position, or they simply take too much time to decide, then rush through their normal pre-swing routine.

Be aware of your situation before your turn to play. It will help you make a better swing, a better score, and have a better day.

64. "I'LL GET TO MY SHORT GAME...."

If you wait until you're happy with your full swing you will NEVER work on your short game, because perfecting the full swing is a life-long quest for everyone, from Ben Hogan, Jack Nicklaus and Tiger Woods on down, and no one is ever completely satisfied with their full swing for more than a few minutes at a time.

Some of my students tell me they don't care about their score, but I never met anyone who was as happy with a seven as with a five.

For the next month, spend fifty per cent of your practice time within 30 yards of the green—putting, chipping, pitching and sand play. Your scores will improve, your enjoyment will increase and you'll play more golf. Improvement in your short game has three benefits: Lower scores, increased enjoyment and improved long game. That's right—the mechanics of striking a solid chip or pitch will reinforce proper swing habits for the full swing. Your hands, arms and body are learning proper movements at low speed.

65. HALF THE GAME

Soon after you started playing you realized that completing a par-72 course as the designer intended would consist of 36 swings with woods and irons and 36 putts. In other words, half the game is on the greens.

So why is it that most players spend their warm-up time hitting drivers, then if they have a few minutes, stop by the putting green on their way to the first tee, roll two or three and think they're ready? The fact that a three-foot putt counts just as much as a 300-yard drive somehow is lost on most of us until after we miss one.

You don't have to be young or strong or even particularly athletic. You just have to apply yourself.

Successful putting can be broken down into four parts plus confidence, and confidence comes from being able to handle the first four. These are:

- The ability to read greens
- A putter that fits you
- Intelligent practice
- Good mechanics

66. MECHANICS
ARE THE FOUNDATION

We've all seen or at least heard of some legendary player who used a rusty putter, had an odd stance, slapped at the ball with his hands—and made everything. The great Bobby Locke hooked all his putts, and was the best of his time. Most of us can probably add a few more stories about good putters who had their own styles, but in this day and age, with even most municipal-course greens being far better than they were even a decade ago, putting mechanics have become fairly standard. Watch any telecast of a PGA Tour event and you'll see that aside from minor variations in style, this is true.

(We're eliminating long putter and belly putter users, because, sad to say, they are usually players, regardless of their over-all skill, who are having trouble with the "normal" flat stick.)

Good mechanics put you in a position to succeed. If you have bad mechanics you are going to have to compensate during your stroke in order to make up for them.

- First, make sure your forearms are under your shoulders, be-cause that's going to help you maintain your swing path.
- Second, make sure your wrists are fully uncocked at ad-dress (both thumbs pointing to the ground—this helps keep your wrists stable at impact.)
- Third, your eyes should be directly over the line of the putt.
- Fourth is your balance. Make sure your hips are over your ankles.
- Now put the book down and check your stance.

Most modern-day putting strokes fall into one of two categories, either straight back-straight through, or "arc" putting, where the putter face stays square to the normal arc the putter swings on based on the lie angle of the shaft at address. Probably 80 per cent of good players are "arc" putters, and 20 per cent are straight back-and-through put-ters. Regardless of which method you use, the basics of the stance are the same.

67. CONFIDENCE

Telling someone to be confident is like telling someone to relax. I don't think you can simply tell someone to relax, or to be confident. They are going to be relaxed or not relaxed, confident or not confident, based on what preceded the present moment.

Confidence is the result of success, and success is the result of good mechanics and good practice habits. Confidence is not simply getting up on the tee and feeling good. You feel good because you've done something previously that was successful. You have to lay this base of success in order to develop confidence.

68. DOES YOUR PUTTER FIT?

As with many mass-produced items, putter manufacturers try to make one or two sizes fit all. In the case of putters, the normal "one size" hardly fits anyone. Most putters come in 35-inch lengths, yet many PGA Tour players today are using 32 or 33-inch putters, with just a few at 34 or 35 inches (This doesn't include belly putters, obviously.)

Technology has found, through camera work, that the only way most of us can set up to the ball properly is with a putter shorter than 35 inches. Much of this depends, obviously, on your height. A longer putter will push you away from the ball so that your eyes can't be directly over it, and your forearms won't be under your shoulders. So if your putter is too long, you are at a disadvantage before you ever take the blade back.

They have also discovered, much too late, that shorter putters have to be heavier, so women, especially, have for many years been at a disadvantage with putters that are too light.

The first step in fitting is to be in the correct address position. The procedure we use is that we have you hold the putter with your elbows against your rib cage, and holding the putter pointing to the sky. Now bend down and lower the putter to the ground. At this point your eyes should be directly over the ball and your forearms should be directly underneath your shoulders. With this setup, you will find the proper length by doing the following:

Once you are in the address position, take the hand that is not your target hand—your right hand for right-handed golfers, left for lefthanders—and let it come off the putter grip. If it hangs parallel to the grip, then you know you are the right distance from the ball. If it hangs closer to your body than the grip, then you are too far from the ball. If it hangs outside the grip, you are too close. Now make the adjustment until your hand hangs parallel to the grip. In most cases you will find the putter is too long. This procedure was developed by well-known Midwest putting instructor Todd Sones.

Once you assume the correct address position with a proper-length putter, have someone check to see if the sole of your club is flat on the ground. If the toe is up, the putter is too upright, which may cause you to pull. If the heel is up, you may push the putt.

Adjusting the lie angle is something best entrusted to a club maker. Or get another putter.

69. READING GREENS

You should start reading a green from about 75 yards, as you approach. See the over-all tilt of the green—right to left, left to right, front to back, occasionally back to front. Looking at it from this distance give you a general overview that may be lost when you are closer.

On the green, look at your putt two ways, first from behind the ball. You can do this just bending from the waist, I don't think you have to get down on the ground. Again, you'll get a feel for left to right or right to left, and you'll get a feel for how much break you will have to play.

The next step, if you're still not certain, is to take a midpoint between the ball and the hole—on the low side. This will confirm the amount of slope that's coming toward you, and also give you a feel for distance and the degree of up or downslope. I think there are also times when you should view it from the opposite side of the hole just to reconfirm, but by looking at it from a distance, from behind and from the midpoint you can get a pretty good feel.

Remember that fast greens break more, slow greens break less. When you have an uphill putt play for a little less break, if it is downhill play for a little more.

The type of grass also plays a role. There are various kinds, but we can break them down into Bent or Poa Annua, both found mostly in cooler climates, and Bermuda, which grows in the Sunbelt. With Bent-grass greens the principal problem is reading the slope and with Bermuda you also have grain to deal with. On Bermuda you may find the slope going right to left, but the grain going left to right. You'll have to favor the grain over the slope, unless the latter is quite severe. For someone coming from Bent to Bermuda, or vice versa, a lot of practice is needed to be comfortable.

The grain in Bermuda greens grows toward the setting sun, and if you're playing on one of these, look at the cup. You will see that the rough edge is the side where you're going against the grain. Another way to find grain on Bermuda greens is to check the color of the grass. If it looks silvery, you're down-grain, If its darker, then you're into the grain. In most instances Bermuda greens putt slower than Bent, and the ball is going to break less. Grain can also be present in Bent or Poa

Annua greens, especially if there is water nearby, as the grass will grow towards the water.

And then, one day when you think you can really read greens, you're going to find a putt that reacts completely opposite to everything that you've read. You weren't wrong—that's just golf.

70. PUTTING PRACTICE

There are two things you are trying to achieve with practice putting. One is proper technique, and the other is feel. Work on technique first, because if your technique is faulty then your "hit" will vary and it is hard to practice feel, because you don't have a consistent strike.

"Regular" Practice

The first thing you do, assuming you have a proper stance and a reasonably well-fitted putter, is make 10 two-footers in a row. This allows you to focus on technique, because you are normally going to make all ten. What is interesting is that most people, when they get to eight, nine and 10, become a little anxious because they know if they miss one of the last three they've got to start all over again.

There are other games you can play to keep your mind occupied. I have my students, after they make the 10 two-footers, drop four balls about six feet from the cup—left, right, above and below. In this way they can practice all breaks—left to right, right to left, uphill and down.

Having done that, and assuming you now have a reasonable stroke, there are two more drills: The first is to putt 10 balls 30 feet from the hole, putting uphill and then downhill, to get a feel for distance. The second is to take two balls and putt around the nine holes of the putting green in a mini-competition, Ball A against Ball B. All of this will take you 25 to 30 minutes, and there is enough variety to hold your focus.

Practice Before Playing

The amount of time you have is important. You may not have time, for example, for 10 two-footers in a controlled and quiet environment. So putt five two-footers.

Then, if you're ready to go to the tee, putt a few 30 footers, because your expectations of success are low—you don't really expect to make these. You're just rolling the ball, getting a feel. What you DON'T want to do is walk off the putting green having just missed a two-footer.

71. PUTT WITH A COIN

Putting has been misunderstood by many for many years. Most people think you hit the ball on the upswing and thus create some sort of topspin.

But testing done with players from the PGA Tour shows that the clubface is actually delofting at impact.

A great way to make sure you are delofting is to throw a coin on the green (use a nickel or a quarter—a dime is too thin), then address the coin and make your putting stroke. If you move the coin, this means you would be compressing the ball at impact. If your putter head glides over the coin that means you are actually adding loft at impact. This is a negative, as it leads to a weaker strike.

It is a simple drill—just throw a coin down on the green or on your carpet at home.. This will help getting you into a good impact position.

72. ANOTHER DRILL

This is a simple one. You can do this on the putting green or you can do it at home if you have a rug long enough.

Take four yardsticks and make a square around the hole, which will put the hole 18 inches from the edges. You can also use a thin string, or four tees, less visually effective, but easier to set up.

Now, from 20 feet, putt 10 balls and get them all inside the square.

Anything that ends up inside the square is going to be less than 18 inches from the hole, and if you can put 10 balls inside 18 inches from that distance, that's pretty good.

When you can do that consistently, the next step is to work on 10 balls from 30 feet, and then 10 balls from 40 feet.

If you can put 10 balls feet inside the square from 40 feet, you're ready for the Tour—at least from a putting standpoint.

73. THE DOUBLE OVERLAP

I learned this back in the 70's when I was working with Jim Flick at the Golf Digest schools. He would teach students to hit short shots with a double- overlap grip. This reduces excessive hand action , which is can be one of the faults of higher-handicap players.

Now we know what an overlap grip is, and double overlap means that you move an additional finger over your other hand. If you are right handed, where you normally have your right pinkie between your left forefinger and middle finger, now take the fourth finger of your right hand and slide it into that slot. You now have two fingers of your right hand over your left hand.

If you practice your short game with that—pitching, chipping, sand play—You will find that your hands work more as a unit and you'll get less breakdown at impact.

I use the double overlap for these shots, and have ever since I learned it from Flick, so I've used it for more than three decades. Two PGA Tour players are known for using it—Calvin Peete did it for his entire career, and Jim Furyk does it today. Furyk uses it with all his shots, including the driver.

74. CHIPS AND PITCHES

It always surprises me when I find someone who confuses the two, so let's remind ourselves:

- In a chip the ball spends most of its time on the ground.
- In a pitch the ball spends most of its time in the air.

We're referring to shots within, say, 40 yards, shots for which you don't need to use a range finder or look at a sprinkler-head marking, the type of shots that enable the PGA Tour players to post under-par scores. These, along with putting and bunker play, are keys to the short game.

If we are to accept the universally held opinion that the Tour players are the best in the world, a look at their 2009 statistics will prove the importance of the short game.

The average Tour player score in tournament play was 71.04—just under par. But the Tour average for hitting fairways was only 63 per cent, and the average of greens reached in regulation was only 65 per cent.

You should be getting a message from this.

If not, then add the following: The "scramble' average—that is "up and down"—was 57.5 per cent, and the average number of putts per 18-hole round was 29.2, or almost seven under the two putts per green allotted by the score card. The primary reason for the low number of putts is the fact that Tour pros chip and pitch the ball close to the hole. So let's get back to chipping and pitching.

When you're approaching your shot, decide if it is going to be better in the air or on the ground. Look to see if you have an obstacle to carry—it could be a bunker or a knob, which will be obvious, or it might be the elevation of the green, which could be higher than the current position of your ball, or the hole might be cut at the back of a two-tier green.

So the pitch shot is anything where you need to carry the ball. The chip shot, a running shot, is everything else. I always putt the ball if I'm within three feet of the green, providing the grass of the apron is even. Outside of three feet, for a chip select your club based on two things: One is going to be the length of the shot, including how much longer grass you have to go over before reaching the green, and two is the elevation of the shot. If it is an uphill shot you are probably going to use a more straight-faced club, because uphill you'll be fighting gravity. If it is downhill you might use a more lofted club to chip because gravity will be helping the ball roll.

Back to pitch shots:

There will be times when you are playing to a two-tier green and the hole is cut on the back shelf. In this situation it will be difficult to run the ball up and include in your calculation how much speed you need to carry the hill and then stop the ball near the cup. If you have 20 feet from the edge of the crown to the hole, then land the ball on the top shelf, because 20 feet is enough for an average to better player—or should I say average to better short game player—to land the ball up there and get it to stop.

If the distance is less than 20 feet you will have to be highly skilled to land the ball on the top shelf and then stop it, so then it might be time to go to Option B, which is to chip the ball.

There are two schools of thought regarding club selection for chips and pitches, one being to use one club for all and adapt that club to the situation, and the other is to use the club that best solves your problem. The one-club method requires feel, and if you have a great sense of feel then go for it, but you will be a member of a distinct minority.

It is hard to live on feel, it is easier to live on mechanics, so I'd suggest you switch clubs in almost all cases because once you develop good mechanics you can change the club, you don't have to change the mechanics. When you rely on one club, you're really changing the mechanics based on feel.

Finally, we should mention the hybrid chip, for which you can use one of your hybrid clubs or a fairway wood (preferably a five wood). When your ball is nestled against the collar of the green and it is difficult to meet the ball squarely with either a putter or an iron, try a putting stroke with a hybrid.

The design of the club head will spread the thick grass rather than get trapped in it, and the loft of the club will give the ball its initial height, enabling it to escape and run to the hole.

75. CHIPPING WITH a PUTTING GRIP

I met the late Paul Runyan, who was known as a great short-game player, when he came to Westchester to meet his old friend Harry Cooper, and when I watched him chip, I saw that he was chipping with his putting grip.

When I asked why, his answer was simple: There are fewer variables.

Runyan explained that "In a putting stroke the wrists don't hinge, and I don't want my wrists to hinge when I'm chipping. So by addressing the ball and chipping with my putting stroke I have less chance of my stroke breaking down."

"It might require a little longer backswing to develop enough leverage," he added, "but I take out one of the variables."

So if you struggle at all with chipping, consider using your putting grip, which for me is for the club to be in the channel between the two muscle pads of your target hand, and also to have your target hand (the one closer to the hole) uncocked. In order to simulate your putting stance, you will also have to have the heel of your chipping club slightly off the ground.

You'll soon be a more consistent ball striker.

76. PITCHING and SAND PLAY

First, let's understand there is a basic difference in what initiates and controls the swing:

Shots within 30 yards of the green should be initiated and dominated by your hands and arms, as opposed to swings for shots longer than 30 yards, where the body becomes the leader.

Pitching and sand shots are forearm shots, and if you think about that for a minute, you will be a better pitcher and sand player. If you are attentive to your target forearm on your backswing, and that controls your backswing, your body will move as the result of the movement of your forearm.

Practicing this will give you the strength and consistency you need to become a good pitcher and sand player.

You want to focus on the target arm—for right handed players your left forearm—swinging up in a more vertical fashion on the backswing, and then your back arm—your right arm in this case—driving the club down on the through swing, down and past your front leg.

Use that feeling for both pitches and sand shots. Think about pitching and sand shots as forearm shots, with your lead arm controlling your upper, backward movement and your trailing arm controlling your down, and forward movement.

For sand there are two phrases I use, FLAT and FACING.

If you can set up taking these two things into account, you'll be a better sand player.

Flat means the club face is facing the sky, maximum loft, and facing means the clubface is facing your target. Too often right-handed people get the clubface pointing to the right of the target, and they get way too open in their stance and as a result have too much loft on their club.

So if you remember flat and facing you'll have the best chance for a good shot.

77. BACK FOOT BACK

This is for players who have difficulty with pitches and/or sand shots, and who tend to hit them either fat or thin.. Most people believe that you should have a slightly open stance when hitting a bunker shot or a pitch shot, and in fact most good players are slightly open.

But most amateurs have a problem with their body getting out in front of their arms far too often when they hit short shots. So what happens is they hit behind the ball because their arms are trailing, or sensing they are going to hit behind it, they rush with their hands and they skull it.

If you set up to the ball in a square fashion and then drop your back foot back, so you're in a "closed" foot position, and practice some pitch shots from this stance, you will be surprised at how solidly you hit them, because what this does is allow your arms to catch up to your body at impact, and that is what you are looking for—your arms and chest to match up at impact.

So drop your right foot back if you are right handed, your left foot if you're left handed. You will hit more solid shots.

78. GREENSIDE BUNKERS

Although we've avoided talking about the swing itself we're going to deal with it here, because the greenside bunker swing is different.

In greenside bunkers you let the body respond to the arms instead of the arms responding to the body, as you do in "normal" full swings.

Use the club you would normally use—a 56 or 60- degree wedge, or in some cases for professionals and very low handicap amateurs, a 64-degree wedge. But if there is, say, 50 feet of green between your ball and the hole you may want to use a somewhat less-lofted club, probably a pitching or gap wedge.

The first step is the get the club 'flat,' which means taking your grip so that the club face is facing the sky at address. This brings the "bounce" of the club—the rounded bottom—into a dominant position, so that the bounce is closer to the sand than the leading edge is, and as a consequence so you won't dig in as much when you swing.

Now, with the face flat, take your stance and make sure the club is facing the target. Next, make sure the shaft is either vertical or leaning AWAY from the ball, as opposed to the "normal '—for other shots—leaning slightly toward your front foot. This allows the face to stay "flat" and facing the target. Any time you get the handle forward you're losing loft and getting the leading edge into a dominant position—something to avoid in bunkers.

Play the ball a little forward of center, because most swings bottom out in the middle of one's stance, so by playing the ball forward you are encouraging yourself to take some sand.

Many students ask "How much sand?" I don't think about how much sand I take, what I do is adjust my ball position to determine how much. Assuming you are going to bottom out your swing in the middle of your body, if you want a lot of sand move the ball forward, if you want a little sand and the ball to run after it lands, move the ball toward the center and you'll take less.

The swing varies from the full swing in the sense that I'd like it to be a little more vertical. So I focus on my target (front) forearm swinging up on the back swing, and I like to make sure I get it at least above hip level. If I do that then I have enough leverage to deliver a good strike to the sand that will compress the sand and push the ball out of the bunker.

On the downswing your trailing forearm drives straight down, and you'll be surprised how hard you can swing if you maintain your balance. Drive that forearm down and past your front foot!

If you get to be a forearm player you'll find that your body responds nicely, so there is some pivot going on, but make sure that in greenside bunkers the body responds to the forearms rather than the arms responding to the body.

V. IT'S ALL IN THE MIND

79. THE GAME IS PLAYED BETWEEN THE EARS

The great amateur Bobby Jones, winner of the "Grand Slam" of all four major tournaments in 1930, said that competitive golf is played on a five-inch field—the space between the ears.

In one sense all golf is competitive, whether you are playing for a major championship or only playing against yourself—possibly the most difficult of all opponents. No other sport offers golf's demanding combination of precise physical techniques and the need to avoid stress while focusing on the task at hand. The ability to perform at your best relates directly to your state of mind and your physiology, and your state of mind has a direct effect on your cardiovascular and muscular systems.

So let's set the scene. You are on the 18th hole with a 10-foot putt to win:

a.   The U. S. Open
b.   Your club championship
c.   A $2 Nassau

In any of these scenarios, tension, and your ability to stay "in the present," are going to play a major role in what you do next. In recent years sports psychologists have become prominent in many athletic disciplines, perhaps most of all in golf because of the mental demands of the game. There is little question that sports psychologists have had a beneficial effect on most of their clients, but they are expensive and those who enjoy a certain celebrity because of their relationship with better-known PGA Tour players are hard to reach.

80. MEET DOCTOR BACCI

As an alternative to a sports psychologist, we've had success at Westchester with a method developed by Dr. Ingrid Bacci that stems from her Mind-Body Training Clinic[3]. It involves your breathing, is easy to practice and to employ in actual play, with the caveat that you will get out of it what you put into it.

Dr. Bacci's method involves the basic use of your breathing mechanism and the simplification of your thought process. Note that by breathing we mean a full abdominal breath, where you take the air into your stomach, until you can feel it expanding, and then contracting, your body to expel the air.

Simplifying the thought process means undoing what most of us have lived with since childhood. We are trained to multi-task almost from the age of four or five, basically when we first undergo formal schooling. The tempo picks up as we get into high school, then college, and if you have a career, the expectations are that you will be able to handle several disparate things at the same time.

The ability to do that will probably make you a successful person, but taking those skills and that mindset into playing golf makes it very difficult, because golf tends to be played, ideally, not only on a single plane in terms of your swing but also on a single plane in terms of your mindset.

You need to develop the ability to be simple, and we're not trained that way. We're trained to be more complex and more sophisticated and golf is not played successfully at that level. That's why sometimes you'll see people who are very simple play very good golf, because they tend to think on a single plane.

The best way to develop that ability, and it's an ability no different than knowing how to hit a tee shot or a bunker shot, is to learn how to be "in the present," when the only thing in your mind is the task at hand—not the weather, not the trophy you might win, not the noise from passing cars, nothing but the shot in front of you. And the only way you can be "in the present" is if you've been there before, and therefore know how to get there.

If I ask you to sit down and focus on your breathing and just count five consecutive breaths, by the third breath your mind will in all probability be off thinking about something else. It's a simple goal—just focus on your stomach rising and falling with each breath. At the outset you probably won't be able to get to five breaths, so that's what you're going to work on. This breathing exercise, a form of meditation, can do a lot for your game.

Commit five minutes per day, five days a week for a month. Find a quiet place where there are no distractions, no interruptions. Take a comfortable seat, with your feet on the ground, and cross your hands over your abdomen. Close your eyes, and feel your hands rise and fall with your breathing. Your mind will wander—that's normal—but each time it does, just gently return it to concentrating on your breathing. Allow your breaths to be deeper, feel your hands rise higher. Your initial goal is 10 sets of five breaths.

Developing this skill is a key to maximizing your performance. So you need to develop it and you need to commit time to it. If you want to maximize your ability, whatever that ability may be, you have to learn to be in the present. You're not going to make a 20 handicapper into a 2 by being in the present, but you're going to be a 20 (if that's what your swing allows) and not a 30. There's also another side effect to being in the present: Your body is actually in a different physiological state—it is much calmer.

Do this every day, and after a few weeks you should be able to get it up to 15 sets of five—and ultimately you'd like to do it for a half an hour. That goal might take you six months to reach. In the meantime, you'll find you're going to be more relaxed when you come out of your brief session—for an hour or two afterwards you're going to be less tense and more focused.

81. TAKING IT TO THE COURSE

Now what do you do with this skill?

Let's suppose you're on the first tee and you're anxious, or you're standing over a fairway shot with a pond on the left and you have a tendency to pull your shots, so your mind goes to the pond, and now you're obviously projecting into the future instead of being in the present.

So take an abdominal breath and two things are going to happen:

First of all you're going to be physiologically more relaxed, and second you're going to be "in the present," so when you make your swing you're not focused on the pond—you've transferred your focus to your breathing and you just go ahead and make your swing. The breathing exercise has not only kept you in the moment, but it also has a positive physiological effect.

Breathing definitely controls your physiology so if you want to be more relaxed when you swing, so the muscles can work in the order they should, breathing will help.

So it's got two benefits, physiological and psychological.

You can also focus on your breathing while you watch others in your group play. This will help you soften your breathing and muscles and help improve your breathing technique.

82. FINDING THE PATH

There are many times on the golf course that we are better than we think we are. The culprit, in this case, is our mind, which tends to limit us—if we let it.

I was playing at the Bonita Bay Club, just north of Naples, Florida, one day, because I wanted to see the facility, and I was paired with a member. I was playing the back tees and he was at the forward tees, and when we got to the ninth hole—he was a man of about 60 and perhaps a 15 handicap and could carry his drives about 190—I said "Why don't you come back here and play with me?"

From my tee it looked as if you had fly it about 170 to carry the hazard and reach the fairway, and he said "I can't hit it that far."

I said "You probably can," and then I said, kiddingly, "If you can't hit it that far, you can hit it down the cart path and then you won't lose your ball," and this guy, who hadn't hit it within 40 yards of his target during the first eight holes, stood up, aimed for the cart path, actually hit the path, the ball bounced a few times and then rolled on to the fairway.

Ben Hogan most probably couldn't have hit the shot even if he was trying, but in order to save his ball this 15 handicapper was able to hit it down that narrow walkway.

One never knows.

VI. FITNESS: YOU NEED IT

83. A NECESSITY

If you are serious about improving, raising your golf-specific fitness level is a must. For some people the lack of flexibility may be the only thing holding you back. The swing, regardless of who is teaching it, is basically a rotational movement and if you can't rotate properly while staying in balance you are the equivalent of being four down on the first tee.

Soon after I became a teaching professional it became apparent that the great majority of golfers past the age of 40—and many of the younger ones as well—couldn't make the swings they wanted to because their bodies wouldn't respond. Every fall we would make an announcement about the availability of one fitness course or another, and these were always met with a resounding silence. When you spoke about it with someone, you could watch them nod in agreement and their eyes glaze over at the same time.

Frank Stranahan, an outstanding amateur in the late 1940's-early 50's, was possibly the first quality golfer to incorporate fitness as part of his routine, and was laughed at by many because of the weights he carried in his luggage. They didn't laugh when he was the runner-up to Ben Hogan at the British Open of 1953 and was one of only three men to break 70 at Carnoustie that year. Gary Player, all of about 5-7 and 150 pounds, started preaching fitness in the late 1950's and today, in his 70's, he is in better shape than many people half his age.

It took Tiger Woods to do it. His workouts have transformed him from a skinny kid to an imposing athlete, and the word athlete is used carefully. You don't fly a golf ball over 300 yards without a combination of skill, strength and flexibility, and now most everyone on the PGA Tour has a formal workout program.

What it boils down to is this:

Whatever else you learn, whatever you practice, if your physical condition is not adequate for the task, you are not going to make a substantial improvement.

Although any licensed physical therapist can review your present fitness level and make recommendations, the increased emphasis of the past decade has brought with it a number of golf-specific conditioning programs, among them Body Balance for Performance (Fitgolf. com) and the Titleist Performance Institute (MyTPI.com).

TPI is by far the biggest and most varied of all the programs, and has been functioning as part of Titleist's business plan for more than a decade. Check the website to see what is available.

We've had the most success, however, with Flexor, a seemingly simple but remarkably sophisticated program that brings, even after the first training session, a small but nevertheless noticeable improvement. When continued on a regular basis, it can lead to marked improvement. It was developed by Frank ("Skip") Latella, who has several degrees in the field of adaptive physical education, and it has been validated at the University of Pittsburgh's School of Medicine.

What the Flexor program (Flexor.com) does is train the brain to send the correct signals, in correct sequence, to the muscles involved in a proper swing. Note this is diametrically opposite to the much-used term "muscle memory," which makes Latella laugh. Muscles don't have brains, he reminds us. There is only one brain in your body, and that's the one sending messages to the muscles.

The Flexor program builds up through progressive levels of training that continue for months. The initial program consists of 12 weeks of simple exercises using a three-foot long styrofoam roll, a large exercise ball and a pair of partially inflated rubber discs about 13 inches in diameter. The exercises are designed to enhance the single core movement key to the golf swing—the rotation of the torso. This is done by putting the body into positions it will assume during a swing, one at a time, and holding those positions for five counts.

There are five positions—lying, seated, standing, on one knee, and in a staggered stance with one foot in front of the other. Each position has four different exercises, making a total of 20 variations, but the basic movement of the exercise is the same in each case. They are done three times a week, require from 15 to 20 minutes, depending on how far along you are in the program, and after 12 weeks you are directed to a maintenance schedule, or you can progress to more advanced drills.

What you are doing, basically, is programming your brain to send the correct signals, in proper sequence, to the muscles that make a golf swing. It does not interfere with your professional's teaching system, since core rotation is the key to whatever he's telling you. Flexor works, with the caveat that you will get out of it what you put into it.

84. STRETCHING

We've said it before, and here it is again: If you work 40 or more hours a week on something other than golf, then being flexible enough is a prime concern. An important corollary to your basic fitness program is pre-round stretching. Whether or not you are in good shape, and whether you are a low or a high handicapper, a little stretching will help. Simply put, it will save a few shots—maybe even more

Stretching before playing also helps avoid injury. Stretching afterward helps increase your range of motion. There are two schools of thought about stretching, one is the yoga school, which is "hold a stretch for 30 seconds," and there's a second school which has come on in the last 15 years called active isolated stretching, which maintains that you should hold a stretch position for five to seven seconds and do five to 10 repetitions of that stretch.

Try to walk to the range, or the first tee, in order to get your body warmed up a little bit, and when you get there first do gentle arm circles. Hold your arms out, left and right, about shoulder height and circle them in both directions, first forward and then backward, about five times. Then put a club behind your back and hook it under your arms straight ahead, turn your shoulders to your right—you won't be able to go too far—hold that to Place your feet about shoulder width apart with your knees flexed, and then, keeping your hips the count of five and do that five times. And then, from the same position, turn to the left, holding each to the count of five, and do five repetitions. This will stretch your lower back.

Then hold two irons, grips together, with the club heads about waist high, and swing the two clubs back and forth gently, about 10 times. Keep your feet flat on the ground.. This will stretch your upper back and shoulders. Then stretch your neck a little. Looking straight ahead, let your chin drop to your chest, and then twist to the right and then to the left, slowly, 10 times. This will stretch your neck muscles.

During the round a few ideas for stretching when you have to wait: Do the club-behind-your- back drill, this will keep your lower back stretched. Also, try this: Put the clubhead in your left hand, your right hand on the grip, hands above your head, then lean to your left, hold until three, and then lean to your right and hold until three. Do three or four repetitions. This will help stretch your sides.

Finally, you should develop a 15-minute stretching routine for your hamstrings, quadriceps, hip flexors, lower back, upper back and shoulders. Do this in the evening, either before or after a hot shower or a warm tub. You will have a greater range of motion than if you stretch in the morning.

85. MUSCLES AND MEMORY— AGAIN

We've heard the phrase "muscle memory" for years, and we assume that when we go on the range and hit balls for two hours a day, five days a week, for weeks on end, that we'll develop proper muscle memory. The idea that muscles have a memory is one of golf's great misconceptions.

The fact of the matter is that there is no muscle memory, there's only brain memory, and it is important that we understand this. What we are really trying to do when practicing is developing brain patterns through repetition. When you succeed in accomplishing this, the brain will trigger the muscles into working in proper sequence.

How do you develop these brain patterns.?

You do it through repetition, and you do it through multiple practice swings, done slowly, and you do many more practice swings than you do hitting the golf ball, so that your brain can develop these patterns,. So when the next person says "I just need to go out there and develop muscle memory," what he really needs to do is understand he is trying to develop a brain pattern, and the brain will absorb the information if it is fed in a repetitious fashion, slowly and consistently.

When I discovered Skip Latella's Flexor program, I soon realized we were on the same wavelength, with the only difference being he was training bodies so they could respond to the brain's commands, and I was trying to train the brain through practice swings, drills, and eventually golf swings.

VII. TECHNOLOGY

86. MODERN TIMES

The essentials are you, the club, the ball and the course. But the world of golf includes any number of "other" things that can help you improve. Here are a few of them, brought to us by the advent of technology into what was originally a game whose tools were hand made, plus some thoughts on different parts of your game.

Golfspeak, that cliche-loaded language we tend to use when discussing some of the game's verities, includes observations that may have been true at one time, but might not be today. Take, for example, the old "It's not the arrow, it's the Indian," or its' cousin, the one that says you can't buy a better game.

They are still valid, but not to the extent they were even 20 years ago. Technology has become increasingly important in the design and manufacture of equipment, it has also become a factor in players' physical conditioning and in course maintenance—in other words, just about every facet of the game.

So now, depending on your ambition and your budget:

You can buy a set of clubs designed for your skill level, your swing characteristics and your physical ability.

You can find the ball best suited to your game.

Your instructor can use video to give you a true picture of your swing, or you can use it yourself.

You can buy a range finder to tell you the exact distance to the hole.

And there are devices such as the launch monitor, the K-Vest, the putting machine, and even such recent innovations as Sonic Golf's System 1, all of which can be helpful.

When golf began more than 400 years ago and for most of the time since, equipment was hand crafted, with the first balls being made of wood, and later on by such arcane methods as stuffing feathers inside a leather pouch.

The first clubs were made by whittling wood into the shapes that correspond, more or less—mostly less—to the clubheads of today, and by blacksmiths forging iron heads one at a time.

Players were given swing advice based mostly on someone's observation of the flight of a few balls, and the links on which they played were maintained by herds of sheep keeping the grass down (and fertilized as well, which may have led to the first discussions about improving one's lie under certain circumstances).

So when technology became involved it reached into four different areas, later to become five:

- Clubs
- Balls
- Instruction, which we can now divide into two parts—the swing, and the new emphasis on player fitness. We've treated fitness separately, since it is a subject unto itself.
- Course conditioning—Improved maintenance has been a major factor in making the game more enjoyable. Former U.S. Open winner Ken Venturi was once asked what he considered to be golf's principal technical achievement of the past few decades. "The lawnmower," he said. Golf courses today are maintained by graduate agronomists and the equipment available to them is highly sophisticated.

Technology, in the form of the first assembly-line manufacturing processes, arrived at the onset of the 20th century, when machine-made balls appeared. Steel shafts showed up in the mid-1920's, although some players—most notably Bobby Jones—continued to use wooden shafts for several years after the introduction of steel.

The late 1960's saw perhaps the greatest advancement in equipment, with the advent of perimeter-weighted, investment-cast clubs and graphite shafts. The perimeter weighting was the brainchild of Karsten Solheim, the former General Electric engineer who demonstrated it first in his Ping putter in the 1960's, and then in his irons, with the Eye2 model becoming the best-selling iron in history. Investment casting is nothing more than the 5,000-year-old "lost wax" method of making jewelry developed by the Phoenicians (and is still in use). It was refined by the aerospace industry in California, along with advanced methods of using graphite sheets in aircraft construction that led to the ultra-lightweight shafts we have today.

In the end, it goes back to the arrow and the Indian. But a look at what technology can do for you is worthwhile, because it can help. There are literally hundreds of devices that are "guaranteed" to cut several strokes, and depending on your particular circumstance, some of them might be useful.

87. ARE YOUR CLUBS RIGHT FOR YOU?

Golf is harder than it should be for at least half the people who play it because of one basic fact:

Their clubs, regardless of age or price, have shafts that are too stiff or their lofts and lies are wrong, or all three.

The evidence we have can be termed anecdotal, as no one has ever checked the clubs of, say, 10,000 players and compared this information with their owners' handicaps. But our staff has been teaching for a combined total of more than 150 years, and we see this almost every day.

There is probably no other sport in which proper equipment is as important and as influential on the results achieved, and it is all the more remarkable because there are no industry standards for such basic elements as shaft stiffness—what, for example, is the frequency of an "R" shaft?—and not even unanimity of opinion on what the loft of a six-iron should be.

It is not surprising people quit the game because they find it too difficult, never realizing it wasn't just their lack of talent, it could well have been their equipment.

The most obvious error is in the choice of shafts, which are the most important component of the club. In most instances people—primarily men—are playing with shafts that are too stiff and too heavy. If you are playing with shafts that are too stiff for your swing speed the club will tend to lag behind you, the body will sense this and get out in front of it. You will then block the shot, or sensing that that club is lagging behind, you will speed up your hands to manipulate the club so that the face is square at impact, and like as not you'll hit a snap hook or a pull.

If you are a low-handicap player you may want to investigate higher-quality steel shafts (which can be two or three times as expensive as regular production models), because this can help your ball flight in terms of both height and distance. In general, however, anyone who swings his driver above 90 miles an hour can use a stiff shaft, anyone above 80 can use a regular shaft, and below-80 players will be best off with a senior shaft. Women whose swing speed is over 70 should use a men's senior flex.

It is easy for players with faster swing speeds to adjust to regular clubs within a few minutes, but practically impossible for slower-swing players to adjust to stiff or extra-stiff shafts. So err on the side of caution. The ball doesn't care about the shaft.

Graphite versus steel is a separate issue. The advantages of graphite are twofold: It is lighter, so it should help your swing speed and also help maintain your position at the top of your backswing. It also acts as a shock absorber, so you're not going to expose your elbows and wrists to as much jarring, which can have a negative effect over time. Graphite does take away some feel, which is why better players prefer steel in their irons, making the trade-off that gives up the lighter weight and the shock absorption.

Lie angle, the manner in which the sole of the iron sits on the ground at address, is second most important. If your clubs have a lie angle that is too flat for you what will happen is your shots will tend to go right (if you're right-handed, left if you're left-handed). And as with shaft stiffness, you'll start compensating with your hands. You can play with clubs that are off one degree, but if they are three or four degrees off the swing compensation necessary for straight ball flight is massive and eventually self-defeating.

Club length is also important, because if you have equipment that is either too long or too short for you, swing compensations become a necessity.

What does this mean in terms of its effect on scoring?

If you are a scratch or low-handicap golfer, little or nothing. Either by accident or design you have clubs that fit your height, weight, physical ability and swing style. If they weren't, you wouldn't play as well as you do.

If you are a 15 handicapper or higher, if the lies on your irons are three to four degrees off and the shafts are too stiff, this could be costing you five to eight strokes a round. They also form an effective barrier to any hopes for improvement because in order to hit straight shots with ill- fitting clubs you have to make what are basically incorrect swings.

The good news is that club fitting has come into its own, and today there is no reason you can't buy a properly fitted set of new clubs, or check a set of used clubs before you buy them to see if they can be adjusted to fit you.

Most private clubs, many municipal and daily fee courses and major golf retailing chains either have fitting equipment or can tell you who in their area can do this. You can also Google the Professional Clubmakers Society, which has members nationwide.

The key to fitting is knowing your swing speed, by which we mean the speed of your driver clubhead at impact. You need some type of launch monitor to determine this, but any good fitter will have one.

So identify your swing speed, get the right shaft flex, have the proper lie angles within a degree, proper length within half an inch and have grips that are the right size for you. All of this can add up to a considerable investment, but they don't get old. The prices of used clubs vary widely, and it is advisable to take any iron set you're thinking of buying to a club maker to check their specifications. He will have a loft and lie machine for measuring, which is also used for bending irons to the desired spec. One note of caution: Investment-cast irons are more difficult to bend than forged irons.

There are various, very expensive, sophisticated steel and graphite shafts on the market, but unless your swing speed is above 100 and your handicap below three, they won't help much. I've seen people of means spend a lot of money on these and I don't think their performance improved five per cent.

88. THE PINGS

Like all teaching professionals, Westchester director of instruction Gary Weir has hundreds of tales from the lesson tee, and this is one of the better ones:

" We Scots have a reputation for being pretty thrifty," he says, "And there are times when we earn it. When I was teaching back home in Edinburgh I had a gentleman come to me for a lesson and even though he said he was a 15 handicap he just couldn't hit it, he could hardly get it in the air, but kept saying 'I'm usually much better than this.'

"Then he whiffed two more and finally said 'I really AM much better than this, but two weeks ago I changed from left handed to right handed.'

"Why did you do that?" I asked.

"I got a great price on this set of Pings."

89. FLEXIBLE IS GOOD

He was in his mid-50's, about 6-3, and maybe 230-240 pounds, a Naval Academy graduate and the CEO of a major retail firm, and when I got to the range for his first lesson he was hitting drives about 170 yards with a 70-yard left-to-right curve.

After watching two of these I asked to see his driver.

It was a stiff-shafted club with an 8.5-degree head and it almost hurt just to waggle it, much less hit a ball, and so I went back to our fitting cart and got a 15-degree senior flex offset driver, with the offset reducing the amount of curve and the senior flex allowing the clubhead to catch up with the shaft at impact. So without saying anything about his grip, his stance or his follow-through, I watched him hit three balls.

The average curve was less than 20 yards and he carried the ball an additional 30 yards, so just by changing his equipment he got a major improvement, which would allow him to enjoy the game more.

A lot of times we get in our own way because we don't know, or because we refuse to open our eyes to the reality. Just by putting a more suitable club in his hands, we were able to change his entire view of the game.

90. THE LAUNCH MONITOR

We don't stock iron sets at our club, because we feel buying irons "off the rack" is a waste of money. If you are going to spend hundreds, or even thousands, for a set they should be fitted to you, and the launch monitor is the device we use to measure the various elements of your swing. After a fitting session we order your clubs from the custom departments of most of the better-known manufacturers. We also do this for drivers and fairway woods.

Our chief fitter, Barry Troiano, is an expert, and he takes about an hour to fit a player properly if he is fitting both woods and irons. So don't expect to walk into a store or a pro shop and walk out five minutes later with the solution to your problem. Many of the major golf retailers have a fitting center in their larger stores.

The launch monitor measures just about everything we need to know about how you hit a golf ball: Your launch angle, club head speed, ball speed, carry, side spin, shot deviation and perhaps most important, something called PTR, or power transfer ratio. This is a measurement of how close you come to hitting the ball in the center of the club face. What this means, basically, is that if you catch the ball on the sweet spot, the distance achieved will be better than someone who has a faster swing speed but has trouble finding the center of the face.

There are several good monitors. We use Zelocity, which also makes mini-monitors that aren't much bigger than a book, and which some dedicated players use for their practice sessions. See Zelocity.com for more detailed information.

91. FINDING THE RIGHT BALL

For practically every golfer short of plus-handicap amateurs and touring professionals, a ball that has more spin is the better choice. Balls with softer covers have more feel and are easier to control around the green, giving you an advantage when it comes to the short game. A possible exception to this might be for high-handicappers who play long, fast-running courses where maximum distance is needed.

Every major manufacturer has a variety of both the high-end "three-piece" balls and so-called "budget" balls, which have two-piece construction and which usually cost from 40 to 50 per cent less per dozen. There was a time when the lower-priced variety were justifiably known as "rocks," but design advancements in recent years have made major improvements in this category.

For the budget-ball price, you can now get a variety of designs that will give you a higher or lower flight, depending on your particular need, plus balls designed with more spin.

Consultation with a PGA professional can help.

92. VIDEO

Camcorders have been a help in making golfers understand their swings, and as such they have been an asset to teaching professionals. Used in conjunction with computers, the results can be archived and either played on a split screen next to the swing of a Tour professional, or can be replayed in a month or two later, after the student has done some work on his game.

There are, however, some great players who had problems with watching themselves swing. Peter Thomson, the Australian five-time winner (and three-time runner-up) of the British Open is rumored to have first seen a videotape late in his career, long after he had established his hall of fame credentials. It is said that he was disappointed in his swing and never wanted to see himself on video again.

A similar case is that of Ralph Guldahl, the best American golfer of the mid-1930's. Guldahl lost the 1933 Open by a stroke when he missed a four-footer on the last hole and won the U.S. Open in 1937 and 1938, the latter by six shots. He won the Masters in 1939 after having been runner-up twice, and won the Western Open three straight years (1936-38) when it was considered a major tournament.

Then he collaborated on a book called "Groove Your Golf," which included a series of photos of his swing taken from the side and also looking down the target line. "I don't remember ever learning to play golf," Guldahl used to say, "It just came from playing all the time."

Now he sat down to study his swing, to analyze it, and to check his various positions in a mirror.

Whatever Guldahl had that made him a winner, he lost it writing the book, and never contended again. He spent his later years as a carpenter in Los Angeles, and then as a club professional.

Then again, if you're not Thomson or Guldahl, you shouldn't worry about it too much. Video can tell you the truth.

93. THE SECRET WEAPON: NEW GRIPS

The only thing that connects you to your club is the grip, a simple, inexpensive piece of rubber or similar material that gets hard and slippery with use and age. This is a sort of creeping disease, as it happens only gradually and you may be unaware of it. But your grip pressure has increased and your game has gone downhill as a result.

The amount of grip pressure you exert is key to making a good swing: If your grip is worn or slick you will do one of two things—hold on too tight, which restricts your wrist hinge, a key component of clubhead speed—or the club will turn in your hands, leaving you an open or closed clubface at impact, the number one cause of misdirected shots.

Touring professionals change their grips several times a year, to make sure they get maximum feel with minimum pressure. If you change them once a year that should be enough. It is a small price to pay for maintaining a key to your swing mechanics.

They will dry out whether or not they are used, so don't think if you are an infrequent golfer the grips will remain pristine. A reasonable alternative, especially for cord grips, is to scrub them with a hard-bristled brush and soapy water every month or so. It only takes a few minutes. Dry them with the grip end down, so that if any water leaked into the small hole in the grip's end it will drain.

94. THE K-VEST

The K-Vest is the best device anyone has come up with to show you, in both numbers and in a series of three-dimensional pictures on the computer screen, what your body is doing during a swing, and how your movements compare to those of PGA and LPGA Tour professionals. You don the K-Vest, make a swing, and the report appears on the computer screen instantaneously.

You are given readouts for seven basic positions: Your pelvis and upper body alignment and posture at address, pelvis and upper body turn at the top, plus positions at the top of the backswing, pelvis movement and upper body movement, bend and side bend, and at impact.

This may seem like an information overload, but the manner in which the data and pictures are presented makes it abundantly clear what body parts need work in order to improve your game. And you can get a printout of the session to study at home. The K-Vest measures five-iron and driver swings and gives you 21 readouts for each of the positions. That's a total of 147 bits of information times two, since a K-vest session covers both clubs.

It may appear overly complicated, but iIn practice it is easily and remarkably revealing of your good and bad points and as a consequence it gives you detailed goals for improvement.

Barry Troiano takes about an hour to do a session. He is also TPI certified, as the K-Vest is a key part of the Titleist performance Institute program. Certified K-Vest instructors can be found on both the TPI website (Mytpi.com) and the K-Vest site (K-Vest.com).

95. RANGE FINDERS

They have become practically standard fare, and come in various shapes, sizes and prices. Some work on a GPS system, other simply show you the distance to the flagstick. They are becoming more and more sophisticated, and as a result have had the unfortunate effect of slowing play when in the hands of high-handicap players who are technologically challenged.

96. SONIC GOLF

Dr. Robert Grober, a Yale physics professor with a low handicap and an inquiring mind, has developed a system called Sonic Golf which converts the golf swing into sound that has a pitch and volume proportional to the speed at which the club head is moving.

If that sounds complicated, go to Dr. Grober's website, Sonicgolf. com, and watch his demonstration. You will see that it does work, and that if you hook yourself up to one of Dr. Grober's devices, the sound will give you the feedback you need to improve your swing.

97. THE PUTTING MACHINE

We use the Tomi, which measures alignment at address, alignment at impact, path at impact, stroke and rotation, shaft angle, impact spot, speed at impact and stroke tempo—in other words, just about everything you need to know about the club you use more often than any other in your bag.

We use the Tomi Pro version, and there is also a Tomi designed for home use that covers most of the above. For more information go to Tomi.com. As with all the electronic-learning assists, it can give you a new look at your game.

98. 25 BALLS

When you are a club pro, you have to prepare yourself for all kinds of situations, some of which you won't find in any manual. Take, for example, when we had a PGA Tour tournament at Westchester. There were a number of years when the Tour officials decided they would use the first hole of our South Course as the driving range, which as so narrow there was room for no more than 25 players at a time.

One year we had a rainy pro-am day, complete with shotgun starts at 7 a.m. and 1 p.m, and we had a limited number of Tour-provided range balls combined with two waves of pros for the practice tee. I told the Tour that if we didn't limit the number of balls for each player that would be unfair to the next wave, so they agreed to limit everyone to 25 balls, and our kids filled the practice bags with that number.

Now here we were—rain, two pro-ams in the early morning and two more in the afternoon (we used both courses, and made an adjustment for the "missing" first hole), a too-small range and a group of professionals who had seldom (if ever) heard the word "no."

Normally the caddies come and get the practice balls, and all of a sudden our staff member who was on the practice tee radioed me and said "Tom Kite's caddy just took two bags."

So I said "Just let him know the limit is one," but they weren't agreeing to it. Kite had just won the U.S. Open (this was 1992)., and this was the week after, and I had to go down to the range and take a bag away from the Open champion. Fortunately I knew Tom, but going down there and saying "Tom, you're limited to 25 balls" was not easy. It all went well, but the job of telling a new U.S. Open winner that he couldn't hit as many balls as he would have liked is something you should avoid if at all possible.

And you won't find it in the "How To" manual.

99. THE LAST HOLE

Now go play, and enjoy it.

Enjoyment will bring you back, and the more often you come back, the more chances you will have to improve.

But you can get back to your improvement program tomorrow.

The problems will still be there—and so will the solutions.

###

Endnotes

1   "The Search for the Perfect Swing," copyright © 1968 by the Golf Society of Great Britain
2   A.S. Barnes and Company, 1957
3   Ingrid Bacci, PhD, is an internationally recognized medical intuitive healer and trainer of self-empowerment and is the author of "The Art of Effortless Living" and " Effortless Pain Relief."

Made in the USA
Charleston, SC
06 March 2011